Flexible Hybrid Work

Flexible Hybrid Work

Matti Vartiainen

Professor (emer.) of Work and Organizational Psychology, Department of Industrial Engineering and Management, Aalto University, Finland

Cheltenham, UK • Northampton, MA, USA

Cover image: Pawel Czerwinski on Unsplash

Published by
Edward Elgar Publishing Limited
The Lypiatts
15 Lansdown Road
Cheltenham
Glos GL50 2JA
UK

Edward Elgar Publishing, Inc.
William Pratt House
9 Dewey Court
Northampton
Massachusetts 01060
USA

A catalogue record for this book
is available from the British Library

Library of Congress Control Number: 2024932702

This book is available electronically in the **Elgar**online
Business subject collection
http://dx.doi.org/10.4337/9781035320103

ISBN 978 1 0353 2009 7 (cased)
ISBN 978 1 0353 2010 3 (eBook)

Printed and bound by CPI Group (UK) Ltd, Croydon, CR0 4YY

Contents

Figures

Tables

Boxes

Preface

Hybrid is something that is formed by combining two or more things
(Merriam-Webster)

But the question is: What are these 'two or more things'?

I am convinced that hybrid work is here to stay. In the future, we will see its many faces. Hybrid work is not only alternating between working at home and in the office. I explain my beliefs to myself by recalling the words of Heraclitus (c. 500 BC), 'It is not possible to step into the same river twice', and the core content of the hybrid concept: 'Hybrid is something that is formed by combining two or more things'. Heraclitus from the past reminds us that change is constant because the material and spiritual world's challenges will not be the same tomorrow as yesterday and today. Therefore, today, we can anticipate future developments by imagining possible futures and their benefits and opportunities, and by recognising the hindrances and challenges of the past. Real organisational practices can be built on their basis. That is what I have tried to do in this book on flexible hybrid work. The idea of flexibility provides mental autonomy to imagine what could be an ideal form of organising work from the human perspective, considering the needs to be fulfilled in work activities. As organisations always exist for some purpose, individual needs and goals must somehow be integrated with these purposes. I believe that this is possible by increasing individual autonomy and self-leadership through organisational flexibility. For this purpose, the concept of flexible hybrid work provides some ingredients for use in design and implementation.

In the traditional socio-technical systems (STS) theory, work systems are considered to be systems in their external environment, continuously reorganising their internal sub-systems to achieve a steady state at a level where they can still perform their activities. However, striving to achieve a steady state is comparable to Sisyphos's task of rolling a boulder eternally to the top of a mountain only to see it rolling down again. Because of a changing environment, organisational goals, and changes in the human mindset, there is no permanent steady state, but a steady striving towards it. This indicates that the quality of the external environment plays a role in the functioning of the work system and impacts upon the required flexible organisational structure and resources. Thus, different environments require different adaptation mechanisms and functional structures. I believe that the present sociomaterial theory supports these starting points by underlining the deep intertwining of digital and social elements and their affordances. In today's 'turbulent fields', dynamics arise not simply from the interaction of the component organisations, but also from the field itself. The dynamics of local and global markets and other external shocks have generated turbulent fields for many work systems: organisations, teams and individuals. Surviving in these environments requires the internal capability of work systems, that is, resources which offer the means to respond to external challenges by being goal-oriented. The approach described above may provide a basis to describe and understand flexibility needs and competencies in today's hybrid organisations, applying new technologies to support remote and teleworking, and distributed working.

For decades, I have followed and participated in the discussion on organisational development from the perspectives of teams and individual workers. A short history of the organisational development of basic-level work shows that in the 1960s and 1970s, Tayloristic individual work was transformed into the work of production groups by enlarging and enriching individual work. The term 'group' was used to mean a group of people in any job who have something in common. Teamwork in the 1990s underlined complementary competencies. For example, Katzenbach and Smith (1993, p. 45) defined a high-performing team as follows: 'A team is a small number of people with complementary skills who are committed to a common purpose, set of performance goals, and approach for which they hold themselves mutually accountable.' It was novel to underline that a team is a highly developed group. Later, virtual teams in the 2000s brought the dispersed membership and the technologies used in communication and collaboration as new features to teamwork. In today's organisations, employees participate in many types of groups and teams; many of them are only temporary structures. The work has become 'group-like'. The development of work at the individual level instead of in groups shows a similar development, from telecommuting to remote work, telework and mobile multi-locality, and finally to hybrid working.

The book is not only based on my experiences of new ways of working but also relies greatly on what has been written about remote and telework before and during the COVID-19 pandemic. This literature dates back to the 1970s telecommuting studies, and includes numerous and rich writings about remote and telework since then. The pandemic that raged especially in 2020–22 produced a rich literature about the impacts of obligatory teleworking from home. My aim has been to lean on empirical studies, and because they are numerous, especially on literature reviews and meta-analyses synthesising empirical studies.

In addition, findings are used from the project Hybrid Work – Challenges, Opportunities and Risks Post-Pandemic, funded by the European Foundation for the Improvement of Living and Working Conditions (Eurofound) (Contract

No. 21-3030-18, project no. 190302). Myself and my colleague Dr Outi Vanharanta participated in this project, analysing the survey results collected in Europe during the pandemic. My warmest thanks go especially to Outi; I also thank Eurofound's project managers Jorge Cabrita and Franz Eiffe.

Hybrid work is a moving target, and today there are variations of it emerging around the world based on local purposes, goals and needs in all kinds of environments, using available resources to configure a local hybrid work model. This is exactly what 'combining two or more things' means.

Otaniemi, Finland, March 2024
Matti Vartiainen, Professor (emeritus) of Work and Organizational Psychology
Department of Industrial Engineering and Management,
Aalto University

1. Introduction to hybrid work

Today, hybrid work is often described as working in person in the primary workplace as well as teleworking from home. This book aims to enlarge the concept of handling present and future work, as more flexible configurations of many other elements in work based on the needs of both organisations and employees.

The discussion, definition and development of hybrid work (HW) started soon after the first phase of the COVID-19 pandemic in the Spring of 2020, and has continued since. This discussion touched on the time after the pandemic and what working life and workplaces would be like. Hybrid work was initially understood from the perspectives of the organisation and the individual as work defined by flexibility in terms of the situation, place and time, where the work is done partly from the employer's premises, and partly from home or elsewhere with the help of digital tools and platforms as a medium for work, communication and cooperation. This resembles the traditional notion of telework. However, today, in 2024, it is still an open question precisely what the elements, content and implications of hybrid work are in practice, at the individual, organisational and societal levels, and whether this form of work reflects an evolution of earlier remote work and telework or a transition to a qualitatively new form of work. The issue is very much under construction. This book offers relevant information for answering these questions, and guidance for implementing remote work policies.

The various new ways of working – such as telecommuting, telework, information and communication technology (ICT)-based mobile work, and global and local online work on platforms – have been continuously implemented over the last several decades, and have therefore already been thoroughly reviewed and discussed. However, it can be asked whether the present definitions and their operationalisations will be valid in today's post-pandemic context. For example, Eurofound (Eurofound, 2015; Eurofound and the International Labour Office, 2017; Eurofound, 2020, p. 1), defined remote work and telework before the pandemic thus: 'Telework and ICT-based mobile work (TICTM) is any type of work arrangement where workers work remotely, away from an employer's premises or fixed location, using digital technologies such as networks, laptops, mobile phones and the internet.'

The definition is comprehensive, although it seems that the COVID-19 pandemic and the experiences of societies, organisations and people in general obliged to telework from home changed the situation, and especially the expectations of how to organise and conduct work flexibly in the future. In addition, developments in technologies such as deepening digitalisation, wider bandwidths, the application of artificial intelligence and virtual worlds, and new tools for collaboration platforms offering online communication and interaction opportunities, and access to knowledge, potentially impact upon how we work from afar and face-to-face in practice. Overall, the question of what hybrid work is, and its elements and features, remains open, as does whether a new concept is needed to understand and develop the reality of working life now and in the future, or whether we can operate using traditional concepts.

The natural experiment during the pandemic changed the scene concerning remote and telework totally, as it obliged large numbers of people to work remotely from home. Before the outbreak of the pandemic, significant differences in the levels of remote work and telework among countries were driven by factors such as profession type, gender, organisation of work, and deep-rooted practices and regulations in everyday use, as well as the management culture in various organisations and countries. As regards working from home permanently, International Labour Organization data (ILO, 2021a) indicate that 7.9 per cent of the global workforce – approximately 260 million workers, including artisans and self-employed business owners – worked from home permanently before the pandemic. Company employees accounted for 18.8 per cent of the total home-based workers worldwide. However, in high-income countries, this number was as high as 55.1 per cent (ILO, 2020a), mainly comprising teleworking employees. A global survey (N = 208 807, from 190 countries) by the Boston Consulting Group and The Network between October and early December 2020 (Strack et al., 2021) showed a global shift to full- or part-time working from home (WFH) models, from an average of 31 per cent before the COVID-19 pandemic, to 51 per cent during the pandemic. There was a considerable variation worldwide among countries (for example, 90 per cent in the Netherlands; 37 per cent in China) and job types (for example, IT and technology, 77 per cent; manual work and manufacturing, 19 per cent). For example, the COVID-19 pandemic in South Korea increased the remote workers to total employees ratio from 0.5 per cent in 2019 to 5.4 per cent in 2021 (Taiwon, 2022).

However, today, employees in many countries are unable or not allowed to work remotely. According to Hatayama et al. (2020), the amenability of employers to allowing employees to work from home increases with the country's economic development level. The authors found job characteristics and Internet access to be important determinants of working from home, although there are differences even between the so-called developed countries.

Overall, the number of people working from home (WFH) and working from anywhere (WFA) is expected to increase and stay high, as is the use of digital tools and collaboration platforms. Barrero et al. (2021) suggested five reasons for the popularity of WFH during the pandemic: better than expected experiences with such work during the pandemic; new investments in physical and human capital; diminished social stigma regarding such work; lingering concerns about crowds and contagion risks; and technological innovations that support remote work. In the future, the increasing use of digital technologies and artificial intelligence (AI)-based software will permeate new fields of work and increase opportunities for flexible arrangements in fields that previously were not yet teleworkable.

BUILDING THE HYBRID WORK FRAMEWORK

The flexible hybrid work concept encompasses the systemic manifestations of hybrid work and its requirements, elements and features. The proposed framework indicates the most critical areas and topics where research results can be applied to practical measures. When implementing a hybrid model, the complexity of the job, its context (that is, physical, virtual and social demands), their reflections on the human mind, and necessary resources (that is, technological, personal, social, organisational and societal), must be taken into account as well as the expected well-being and productivity outcomes. When it comes to potential developments in the future, it has been asked (Jain et al., 2021) whether intelligence augmentation (IA) can pool the joint intelligence of humans and computers to transform individual work, organisations and society. Hybrid work can take many forms, depending on the job and its characteristics, the specific operating environment and hybrid work arrangements (for example, location, schedule, hours), the work process and its management, human acceptance, and the impacts on well-being.

STRUCTURE OF THE BOOK

Throughout the book, flexible hybrid work potentials are studied and reviewed using empirical studies from flexible work literature, such as traditional remote work and telework literature. In addition, the evidence from the natural experiment during the COVID-19 pandemic is used, as it produced an extensive literature (Vartiainen and Vanharanta, 2023). Thus, the chapters mainly refer to the conceptual and empirical literature on traditional remote and telework, experiences gained during the pandemic, and future visions of the author.

Chapter 2, 'Flexibility paradigm', introduces flexibility as the fundamental paradigm and concept underlying hybrid work, and discusses flexibility from the perspectives of the organisation, social relations and individual autonomy.

Chapter 3, 'Hybrid Work and Its Elements', addresses the first objective of this book by discussing the concept of hybridity and describing the main elements, sub-elements and features of hybrid work, drawing on existing remote work and telework literature, and the definitions of hybrid work operationalising them. The chapter introduces a preliminary description of the concept of hybrid work.

Drawing on an empirical study, Chapter 4, 'Towards Flexible Hybrid Work', focuses on how hybrid work has been addressed in national policy debates in Europe, among governments and social partners, and at the company level.

Chapter 5 is 'Potential Hindrances and Challenges', and Chapter 6 'Potential Benefits and Opportunities', related to remote work and telework. They identify the expected hindrances, challenges, benefits, and opportunities in the country reports to understand what should be considered when designing hybrid work schemes.

To identify and discuss success factors for HW implementation, Chapter 7, 'Design, Implementation, Adjustment, and Crafting Hybrid Work', reviews the literature on conditions for successful telework, and presents findings regarding how European organisations are currently implementing or planning to implement hybrid work.

Chapter 8, 'Management and Leadership', illustrates the differences between control-based and trust-based leadership styles in hybrid work.

Finally, Chapter 9, 'Future Hybrid Work', presents the book's conclusions and some views about the future.

2. Flexibility paradigm

FLEXIBLE WORKPLACE

The discussion on workplace flexibility started in the late 1990s and early 2000s, from two perspectives: the organisational and worker perspectives (Hill et al., 2008). The *organisational perspective* emphasises flexibility on the part of the organisation, with only secondary regard to workers. The *worker perspective* primarily emphasises individual agency in the context of organisational culture and structure. There has been a long debate characterised by these two perspectives (Lewis, 2003, p. 2): one considers flexible working as a productivity or an efficiency resource and a strategic issue for organisations; and the other perspective emerges from the work–life literature depicting flexible working initiatives as tools for reducing work–family conflict and enhancing work–non-work integration as resources. From the point of view of the market economy, flexibility is an issue of the *neoliberal economic doctrine*, which aims at the constant accumulation and renewal of financial capital. The well-known sociologist Richard Sennett (2006) called it 'flexible capitalism', based on the global dispersal of investment, production and recruitment of labour, allowing for greater flexibility in the accumulation of capital, the production process and the organisation of labour. Critical voices claim (Tessarini et al., 2023) that by the 'flexibility paradigm', capitalism emerged to renew itself to meet the demands of changed production conditions in the global context. Accordingly, several changes are applied to labour, based on the logic of, and discourse about, flexibility; this is done to enable companies to effectively meet market demands, maximise their gains and define management strategies. Chung (2022) argues, when explaining the flexibility paradox phenomenon, that 'flexibility' and 'freedom' at work are just examples of how power has moved from a disciplinary society to a society of control. She argues that like the theory of the 'entrepreneurial self', capitalistic ideas of productivity, performance and profit have now been internalised by workers as their drive and passion. Workers are increasingly made to organise their life in an 'entrepreneurial' manner, where they need to transfer their labour potential into concrete performance. That is, workers manage themselves 'autonomously' without the need for direct managerial control. In the sense mentioned above, flexibility is an ideologically loaded concept behind different worldviews.

Flexibility can also be seen as a more neutral phenomenon. It emerges value-free during crises, turbulences and transition periods calling for resilience, when a reactive, adaptive style is insufficient to meet contextual uncertainties and challenges. Therefore, readiness for change, anticipation, proactivity and renewal are needed. As for the future, it is also possible that the need for flexibility is a transient phenomenon that has appeared during a transition from 'old normal', for example, remote work and telework, to a new, more structured, and stabilised flexible 'new normal', for example, hybrid work.

Numerous recent studies based on representative workforce samples (e.g., Eurofound and the International Labour Office, 2017) show that many aspects of working life are changing. The COVID-19 pandemic further accelerated these changes. More flexibility is needed than before in organising and completing work. Therefore, flexibility is necessary for many operations, incorporating individuals, teams, management, networks and whole societies. It is beneficial to acknowledge the differences between these levels of operation and to distinguish how flexibility manifests in them in practice. For example, in their review, Kossek and Lautsch (2018) show that different types of flexibility are perceived differently in different professional groups. They claim that providing employee control over scheduling variation (flexitime) may benefit lower-level workers the most, yet many lack access to this flexibility form. Flexibility to control work location is rarely available for lower-level jobs, but benefits middle- and upper-level employees if individuals can control separation from work when desired, and self-regulate complexity.

In addition, there may be some *work culture differences*. Masuda et al. (2012) surveyed 3918 managers from 15 countries, classified into Anglo, Asian and Hispanic clusters. Managers from the Anglo cluster were more likely to report working in organisations that offer flexible work arrangements than managers from other clusters. For Anglo managers, flexitime was the only type of flexible work arrangement with significant favourable relationships with the outcome variables, that is, work-to-family conflict, job satisfaction, and turnover intentions. For Latin Americans, part-time work is negatively related to turnover intentions and strain-based work-to-family conflict. For Asians, flexitime was unrelated to time-based conflicts, and telecommuting was positively associated with strain-based work-to-family conflicts.

From the viewpoint of employers and employees, flexibility is a controversial issue. It represents different things to different parties, and potentially creates disputes between them, social partners in general, and individuals' work–life balance. The controversy arises from the question: who decides and controls the prerequisites of flexible practices? The challenge is finding a balanced solution that serves individuals' needs and self-control, and enables flexible working arrangements dictated by the company's objectives and the specific circumstances of such work.

Next, different forms of flexibility are discussed from the organisational and individual viewpoints. In this book, hybrid work is understood as a flexible interplay of various elements, and an adaptive form of work based on what tasks need to be done *in situ*. Therefore, it is beneficial to first describe flexible work approaches in more detail.

FLEXIBLE ORGANISATIONS

From an organisational perspective, the goal of flexibility is to enable the organisation to adapt to rapidly changing demands placed on the organisation from either internal or external forces (Hill et al., 2008). Flexibility comes in many forms. For example, Korunka (2021, pp. v–vi) distinguishes four forms of workplace flexibility: organisation, work relations, time and location. In addition, social relations are flexible. These forms of flexibility are interrelated, and each of them can be practised in different manners. For example, the flexible use of time and location (spatial-temporal flexibility) in work arrangements is often used to arrange hybrid work.

Flexibility in Organisation

Organisational flexibility refers to *functional flexibility* (Atkinson, 1984; Reilly, 1998) that is typically sought by restructuring work; reallocating tasks, reorganising employees, implementing job rotation and expanding roles; enriching opportunities, turning individual work into group work; recruiting new employees; increasing competencies; and adopting tools, technologies and physical premises. There are also several other practices involved in the principles of agile management. For example, project work, which until a few decades ago meant only narrowly defined projects, is today a widely used form of work management. Temporary projects and teams – for example, fast teams – have permanently replaced the conventional line structure within and across many organisations (Tannenbaum et al., 2012). Typically, temporary teams execute a single task or, at most, a few tasks with a definite deadline or a finite time limit to accomplish their goal (Bell and Kozlowski, 2002; Saunders and Ahuja, 2006). An example of a flexible organisation unit is a temporary, virtual team (VT) collaborating via computers within multi-site and multinational organisations. Organisations are increasingly adopting multi-team systems, where knowledge workers are concurrently members of multiple temporary teams (Wageman et al., 2012). The platform economy has broadened the options to arrange flexible work globally, including contracting, platform work (for example, online freelancing), digital labour (for example, micro-tasking and gig work), and nomadic work (Dunn et al., 2023).

Ancona et al. (2021) characterised the changes accelerated by the COVID-19 pandemic concerning team evolution. Team membership changes frequently as part-time members come and go, and suppliers and other stakeholders begin to become members. This implies that employees have multiple memberships in teams. Crossing fuzzy organisational boundaries often leaves individuals with different perceptions of who is on the team. When fuzzy boundaries are crossed, the focus on internal configuration and dynamics shifts to a focus on both internal and external dynamics. The role of technologies changes as well, and their role as necessary tools grows. The organisation as the context also tends to be changed, to the ecosystem as the context.

Flexibility in Work Relations

'Numerical flexibility' (Atkinson, 1984; Reilly, 1998) refers to the ease of increasing or decreasing the number of employees; for example, using an external workforce. This is called 'contractual flexibility' (Tessarini et al., 2023), which covers the forms of contracts and wages of workers, whether informal and/or precarious. Therefore, it configures a working relationship between an employer and an employee. Triggered by the 2008 economic crisis, many permanent work contracts with benefits packages were replaced by temporary and part-time work contracts using temporary staff or an 'expanded workforce' (Kane et al., 2021). An extreme form of such contracts is 'work on demand', that is, a 'zero-hours contract' where employees only work when needed, and do so hourly or daily. Many companies have also moved from permanent contracts to labour leasing contracts and outsourced workforces. In the most extreme global form of such developments, in the 'gig economy' and labour platforms, people worldwide work on a pay-per-piece basis, with neither job security nor traditional employment benefits. While such contracts might offer positive opportunities for some workers (for example, in low-income countries), they result only in high levels of uncertainty for many others. For employers, this kind of 'financial flexibility' (Atkinson, 1984) allows wages and associated benefits to rise and fall with economic conditions such as service demand. It also refers to the remuneration structure, which replaces wage rigidity with alternatives such as varying remuneration based on productivity and bonuses.

Figure 2.1 illustrates the types of employment relationships from the perspectives of the individual worker's work life cycle. The organisation is seen to be constituted from the core workforce and a contingent workforce, such as temporary external workers and freelancers from whom labour input is purchased. One might argue that what is being witnessed here is a digitalisation of the classic core–periphery workforce model articulated by Atkinson (1984). Contingent and autonomous jobs are called 'flexible' (see, e.g., Eurofound, 2015). Demand for increased flexibility has resulted in new forms of employment worldwide. These have transformed the traditional one-to-one relationship between employer and employee. This development was anticipated in an early study on the virtual workplace (Crandall and Wallace, 1997), where its blended workforce was divided into full-time regular, temporary, and contract-based employees. From the organisation's perspective, the core workforce consists of workers indispensable to the organisation and in a permanent, full-time employment relationship, with expertise, know-how and professional competencies. The core workforce is supplemented by the contingent workforce in a looser relationship with the organisation, performing routine wage work of lesser value to the organisation. Contingent workforce participants, compared to those in the core workforce, are more often in atypical, temporary employment relationships, characterised, for example, by part-time employment and zero-hours contracts. The freelance workforce is characterised by an occasional, results-based relationship with the contracting organisation. The workers are not the organisation's workforce, but, for example, employed by a subcontractor or a work lease enterprise. They also include freelancers, consultants and contract workers. A fixed-term contractual nature applies to almost all occupations. Many tasks are seasonal (peak periods and seasons, night and weekend work, substitutions, and so on).

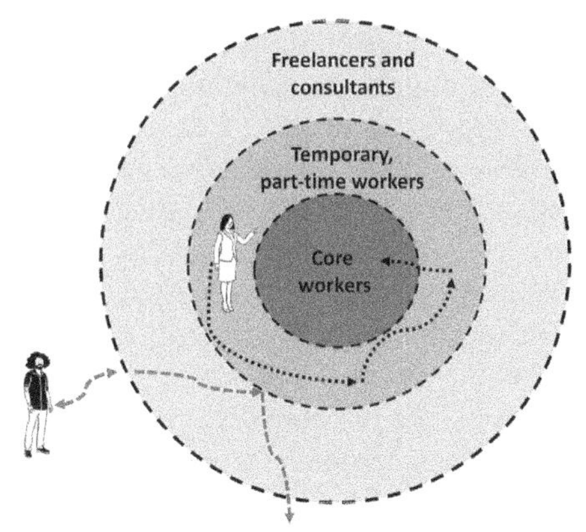

Source: Based on Atkinson (1984, p. 29).

Figure 2.1 *Types of employment relationships from the perspectives of an individual worker and an organisation*

It has long been acknowledged (e.g., Tregaskis et al., 1998) that both the concept and practice of flexibility are controversial issues, especially regarding work relations in the labour market (Reilly, 1998). For example, a manager may see a part-time worker as a valuable source of flexibility as they provide work input when needed. In contrast, from the point of view of a typical part-time worker, this may appear inflexible, because they need to fit other aspects of their life, such as education and family time, around such work. Accordingly, flexibility in time and location, and ways of adaptive organising, include opportunities, enablers and benefits, and challenges and hindrances, to organisations and their employees.

Flexibility in Social Relations

In addition to the above types of flexibility, the COVID-19 pandemic revealed other critical types of flexibility, primarily related to social relations: that is, meeting people by chance or intentionally, and obtaining advice, help and support. *Social flexibility* is the ability to combine in-person synchronous contact with virtual synchronous and asynchronous contact. Working face-to-face with others is beneficial because of the ability to ask others for immediate advice, help and support. In addition, friends and family are critical social resources for overcoming hindrances and challenges at work. This is also possible online, virtually. However, a Microsoft study (Yang et al., 2022) showed that firm-wide remote work caused the collaboration network of workers to become more static and siloed during the pandemic. The boundaries may be a recurring issue with hybrid work in the future. Forced telework from home during the pandemic broke down the flexible mixture of face-to-face and remote solo work, and collaboration with peers and managers. However, simultaneously, many workers' family ties were strengthened. And the work days of many teleworkers became blurred, as there was no specific time or place for the work to start or end. People could work all day in solitude, or in asynchronous or synchronous collaboration with others online.

A now traditional way to increase social flexibility in work-related interactions between two or more people is teamwork, that is, individuals working interdependently towards a common goal and viewing themselves as a team (Hackman, 2003). The virtual team (VT) concept added new meaning: a VT is a dispersed group of people who work interdependently with a shared purpose across space, time and organisational boundaries, using technologies (e.g., Lipnack and Stamps, 2000). However, mediated interaction makes collaboration more challenging, such as the interaction and social relations between VT members and their leaders.

Social relations at work are under pressure from the transformation to hybrid work. This challenge means that in a hybrid work system the forms and means of social interaction must be stabilised in some way. How can face-to-face and virtual meetings, and synchronous and asynchronous work, be balanced? The nature of the organisation is also expected to change. Some researchers (Ancona et al., 2021) claim that the COVID-19 pandemic disrupted and radically changed some aspects of collaboration; previously stable teams were changing to dynamic teams regarding their membership. Team membership frequently changes as part-time and part-cycle members come and go, and as membership changes to customers, suppliers and partners. Clear social boundaries become fuzzy because of the fluidity of teams, often leaving individuals with differing understandings of who is on the team. Ancona et al. claim that the internal focus of a team is changing to both internal and external focuses, because the external context requires more attention than before, and requires balancing multiple memberships. Social demands naturally increase the psychological pressure on individuals who face challenges such as fragmented attention, task switching, conflicting demands and work overload. On the organisational level, such developments are prompting organisations to switch from a team-based orientation to an ecosystem of teams collaborating across organisational boundaries towards a common, overarching goal.

Flexibility in Time

This is also called working time or *'temporal flexibility'* (e.g., Van Eyck, 2003), or flexitime. Flexitime involves building flexibility into an employee's work schedule. Temporal flexibility concerns the following time-related issues: when something happens (timing), how often (time frequency) and for how long (duration). Continuity of time – that is, the ability to leave work for a certain period using the vacation policy (Kossek and Lautsch, 2018) – is also an important aspect from the perspective of permanence versus temporality when adapting to contextual demands and available resources at work. For example, temporal flexibility ranges from flexible time schedules – that is, schedule flexibility, usually with core times where employees need to work in their default workplace – to part-time work and trust-based working hours. In this last case, fixed work durations and schedules are dropped, and work is regulated by agreed-upon and monitored work targets. For example, working hours may be reduced when product or service demand is particularly low, a strategy commonly used in restaurants. Flexible working time arrangements can include, for example, flexitime, term-time working, part-time or reduced hours, job sharing, career breaks, family-related and other leaves, compressed work weeks, and teleworking. Temporal flexibility very much influences the types of work relations.

Temporal flexibility is a standard feature of remote work, telework (White et al., 2003), and hybrid work. Two critical issues in deciding the type of flexible hybrid work are, first, who – the employer or the employee or their representatives – are authorised to decide what hours, days and weeks are permissible for teleworking; and second, what hours and duration of work are required each day. Research on how people in organisations manage their time, and what its effects are, highlight some critical issues. Claessens et al. (2007, p. 262) defined time management as 'behaviours that aim at achieving an effective use of time while performing certain goal-directed activities'. In terms of behaviour, this includes being aware of time, and planning and monitoring the use of time while working. Based on 32 empirical studies, they found that time management behaviour was related to perceived control of time, job satisfaction and health; and negatively to stress. The relationship between work and performance was not clear. It was possible to enhance time management skills through time management training, but this does not automatically transfer to better performance.

Flexibility in Location

Location or *spatial flexibility* in organisations refers to intra-organisational mobility between two or more locations of an organisation, or mobility between two organisations. It allows workers to choose where work-related tasks are completed, and is often referred to as 'flexplace' (Hill et al., 2008). 'Working from anywhere' (WFA) during the pandemic helped workers and firms to reap the benefits of geographic mobility to mitigate the negative impacts of the pandemic. Opportunities to use this kind of flexibility on the individual level depend on the needs of one's current situation, the nature of one's work, and company policy. For example, a maintenance crew must be mobile and go to distant work locations near their customers. The same applies to temporary agency workers. An employee's willingness and need to telework from home and other locations vary depending on their assignment, tasks, working conditions and family situation. Flexible work arrangements may require different physical spaces for home and other working locations when used as workplaces.

Choudhury (2022) suggests a broader concept of geographic mobility to include within-country, cross-border, inter- and intra-firm geographic mobility, and permanent and temporary moves. His comprehensive literature review shows that geographic mobility of high-skilled workers can create value for individuals and firms through knowledge transfer and recombination, social capital transfer, skills development, and resource seeking, among others. However, four types of frictions can constrain geographic mobility or result in costs to the individual during or after relocation (Choudhury, 2022, p. 259): (1) 'regulatory frictions', that is, legal limitations on mobility at the international, national, or local level; (2) 'occupational/organisational frictions', that is, job- or firm-specific barriers to mobility; (3) 'personal frictions', that is, the interpersonal, familial or social factors that limit mobility; and (4) 'economic/environmental frictions', that is, financial and other macro-level impediments to mobility. These frictions can be mitigated (ibid., pp. 282–284) by: (1) awarding geographic flexibility to workers; (2) focusing on temporary co-location of workers; and (3) leveraging place-based policies. By awarding geographic flexibility, the worker can relocate to their preferred location. Another practice, fostering temporary co-location among workers, instead of requiring workers to move to a firm location permanently, is another way in which organisations may mitigate the adverse effects of mobility frictions. This is often practised today in some types of hybrid work. In addition, by leveraging place-based policies, organisations can create business models, for example by moving from a higher cost of living to a cheaper location, enabling value creation for workers facing personal or economic frictions at their current location. All three of these practices could create value for both an employee and an organisation.

Spatial flexibility was implemented in some organisations decades ago, during the early days of telework, but usually only for small numbers of telecommuting employees (Nilles, 1976). In traditional telework, employees had their primary workplace and a clearly defined second workplace, usually in or near their homes. More recently, facilitated by digital mobile technologies, workplace mobility has undergone significant changes for some, with the idea of a default workplace, such as a main office, being abandoned. Work may now be performed anywhere (WFA) and usually at any time. In remote work and telework, an employee's physical location is the main criterion for categorising basic types of workplaces and work. It is also an essential element in different types of hybrid work. A critical issue in this kind of flexibility is who or what makes the ultimate decision regarding the location where the work takes place.

Individual autonomy concerning where to work has a long history. In the book *The Third Wave* by well-known futurist Alvin Toffler (1980), this location-based interpretation of autonomy was anticipated and realistically described 50 years ago. Based on the work by Nilles et al. (1976), Toffler envisioned a new production system that would shift millions of jobs out of the factories and offices into homes and local work centres (today, 'hubs'). Numerous terms illustrate an individual's ability to work from a place other than an office or company premises (e.g., Allen et al., 2015). These include telecommuting, telework, remote work, home-based work, flexible work, distance work, multilocational work, mobile work, and even online work and crowd work. Historically, there has been a slight difference between telework and remote work concepts. The difference stems from the development and use of information and communication technologies (ICTs) and the locations of workplaces. According to the International Labour Organization (ILO, 2020b, p. 6), the fundamental difference between telework and remote work is that a teleworker uses personal electronic devices while working remotely.

Estimates of the exact numbers of remote work and telework types vary due to different ways of collecting data and formulating the questions that measure them in surveys. For example, Kässi et al. (2021) estimated the size of the global online freelance population during the pandemic by gathering data from globally relevant online freelance platforms and using public data sources. According to them, 163 million freelancer profiles were registered on online labour platforms globally in 2021. They conclude that today, online workers represent a non-trivial segment of labour that is clearly growing, but still spread thinly across countries and sectors. Such hybrid work arrangements may grow in the future. Table 2.1 shows the main types of individual remote work and telework in different locations.

The goal of workplace flexibility from the employee perspective is to enhance the ability of individuals to meet all their personal, family, occupational and community needs (Hill et al., 2008). The flexibility of what, where, when, how and for how long is closely related to personal autonomy, a basic human need. Self-determination theory (Deci and Ryan, 2012) suggests that all humans have three basic psychological needs underlining personal growth and development: autonomy, competence and relatedness. The need to be autonomous influences goal setting, what is valuable at work, decisions about what actions to take, tool selection, the location and time of work, collaboration, and voluntary initiative. Van Yperen et al. (2014) found that the perceived personal effectiveness of blended working – that is, time- and location-independent working enabled through ICT – depended on the strength of employees' psychological need for autonomy. Specifically, the perceived effectiveness of both time-independent and location-independent working was positively related to individuals' need for autonomy at work. However, it was negatively related to their need for relatedness and structure. It is concluded that satisfying these basic needs requires flexible ways of organising work to consider individuals' needs, strengths and available resources.

INDIVIDUAL FLEXIBILITY

Workplace flexibility from the *worker perspective* (Hill et al., 2008, p. 152) refers to 'the ability of workers to make choices influencing when, where, and for how long they engage in work-related tasks'. To this must be added the ability to decide what to do. The goal of workplace flexibility from the worker's perspective is to enhance the ability of individuals to meet all their personal, family, occupational and community needs. The definition's essence is the ability to choose the core aspects of everyday work life. Therefore, controlling own actions and autonomous decision-making concerning work–life conditions are the enabling elements of individual flexibility.

Table 2.1 Definitions of traditional remote and telework

TYPE OF REMOTE AND TELEWORK	DEFINING FEATURES
Remote work	Work arrangement in which an employee resides and works outside the local commuting area from the perspective of their employer's worksite (e.g., Mokhtarian, 1991). Remote work is a comprehensive concept and does not require visits to the primary workplace or the use of personal electronic devices, thus allowing many types of locations for work, and it can involve mobile work. A remote worker can be self-employed or dependent on an employer. It is 'working anywhere'.
Telework	Wholly or partially carried out at an alternative location rather than the default place of work, and personal electronic devices (that is, telecommunications) are used to perform the work (e.g., Eurofound, 2020; ILO, 2020b). A teleworker can be a self-employed or a dependent worker. Teleworkers who use multiple locations are called mobile multilocational workers (Andriessen and Vartiainen, 2006; Lilischkis, 2003, p. 3) or mobile teleworkers (Hislop and Axtell, 2007, 2009). Mobile employees spend some paid work time away from home or their primary workplace, for example on business trips, in the field, while travelling, or on a customer's premises.
Home-based telework	Occurs at home using electronic devices. Permanent teleworkers spend over 90 per cent of their work time working from home. Supplementary teleworkers or regular teleworkers spend one full day per week working at home. Occasional teleworkers work from home at least once every four weeks (e.g., ILO, 2020b).
Home-based remote work	Carried out at home or from home. Home-based workers do not necessarily use electronic devices. They can also work at home permanently, regularly or occasionally.
Digital online telework	A common form of employment across the globe that uses online platforms to enable individuals, teams and organisations to access other individuals or organisations from anywhere and at any time to solve problems or provide services in exchange for payment (e.g., Berg et al., 2018).

Source: Based on Vartiainen (2021, p. 3).

Autonomous Action Regulation

Morgeson and Humphrey (2006, p. 1323) suggested that *autonomy* reflects how much a job allows freedom, independence and discretion to schedule work, make decisions and choose the methods used to perform tasks. Thus, autonomy includes three interrelated aspects centred on freedom in work schedule, decision-making and work methods. In addition, individuals may also have autonomy in deciding what they do (work task autonomy), and where they do their jobs (location autonomy). In summary: autonomous action regulation enables flexible ways of working based on an individual's need, ability and opportunities to make choices and influence what is done, where, when, how, and for how long work-related activities are carried out.

As shown above, flexible working arrangements are numerous. For example, de Menezes and Kelliher (2011) listed a wide range of these arrangements in their systematic review[1] allowing employees to vary the amount, timing or location of their work. For individuals, flexibility extends beyond work to the rest of life, especially in hybrid work. Kossek and Lautsch (2018, p. 10) defined work–life flexibility 'as employment-scheduling practices that are designed to give employees greater work–life control over when, where, for how long, or how continuously work is done'. Control over 'when' enables adjusting work starting or ending times, or working a schedule as in flexitime and using a compressed work week. 'Where' allows controlling and adjusting the location of work such as flexplace, telecommuting, remote work, hotelling and mobile work. 'For how long' concerns control over how long they work, which they may do through working only a restricted set of hours, as in part-time or reduced-load arrangements. Finally, the control of 'continuity' of work refers to the periodic interruption of work, including sick or parental leave. Whereas employees' autonomy concerns their discretion over their working tasks, managerial autonomy is the ability and opportunity to adapt to situations concerning time and scale in response to business decisions. In hybrid remote work or telework, autonomy often concerns discretion regarding where to work, and scheduling.

Paradoxes of Individual Flexibility

The *autonomy paradox* (Mazmanian et al., 2013) or *flexibility paradox* (Chung, 2022) appears on the individual level when an autonomous and self-managing employee always works voluntarily and everywhere, often with negative impacts on work–life balance, well-being and health. The digitalisation of information, and the access to it and virtual work, enable asynchronous communication, allowing work performance at any time and place. This makes controlling working conditions and actions more demanding, potentially leading to stress and exhaustion. For example, Kubicek et al. (2021, p. 20) argue that increased cognitive demands of flexible work may have ambivalent individual impacts. They can increase cognitive efforts, strain employees and promote work–home conflict. However, they may also help employees to learn new skills and competencies, because cognitively demanding work can stimulate learning at work. This could foster employees' cognitive flexibility, increase work motivation, and support work–home enrichment. Solving this dilemma requires conscious self-control. The challenge is to find a balanced solution that serves individuals' needs without jeopardising their health, and their mental and economic well-being, and enables flexible work arrangements dictated by organisational objectives and specific situations and circumstances in its search for resilience.

Studies on the 'dark side' of autonomy have shown that although flexible workers record higher levels of job satisfaction and organisational commitment than their non-flexible counterparts, there is evidence that those who work flexibly – that is, work remotely from home for part of the working week, or doing reduced hours – experience work intensification (Kelliher and Anderson, 2010). Kelliher and Anderson proposed that employees respond to the ability to work flexibly by exerting additional effort to return benefits to their employer. Therefore, flexibility may have detrimental effects on the individual level. Both autonomy as a resource, and performance as an outcome, can be curvilinearly linked: 'too much' autonomy can result in increased stress because of an associated increase in effort. This paradox has given rise to a debate about whether regulations on working hours are needed to ensure the 'right to disconnect' (Eurofound, 2021).

Mazmanian et al. (2013) observed in the context of mobile technology use in workplaces that although the individual use of mobile email technology offered location flexibility, peace of mind and control over their interactions in the short term to knowledge workers, it also intensified collective expectations regarding their availability, thus increasing their work activity and reducing their ability to disconnect from work. This phenomenon is called the autonomy paradox. Chung (2022) refers to this phenomenon as the flexibility paradox, arguing that when employees have more autonomy and control over their work, they work more hours and in more places. Empirical studies, for example, show that teleworking from home during the pandemic frequently increased feelings of conflict between work and family rather than improving workers' work–life balance. Chung states that this pattern of exploitation was also gendered: women's unpaid working hours increased, because the time they spent on housework and childcare increased, in adherence with the social norms around their roles as caregivers.

Flexibility is also a paradoxical issue from managers' perspectives. When a manager tries to apply flexibility in managing business complexity and uncertainty, reorienting the organisation and structuring decisions in different functions of the organisation, hurdles can become apparent when flexibility initiatives are realised in practice. For example, lower and middle managers seek workable strategic advice, and may perceive it differently than top management. The paradox is also related to managerial flexibility, which refers to the ability to adapt to situations regarding time and scale in order to take advantage of business decisions.

Shukla et al. (2019) concretise the paradoxes related to *management flexibility*, such as when a manager tries to apply flexibility in managing business complexity and uncertainty, reorienting the organisation or structuring decisions in different functions of the organisation. The paradox appears when benefits, concerns and hurdles are noticed in implementing flexibility initiatives. Shukla et al. (2019) identified three types of managerial paradoxes in their literature review. The first paradox concerns the benefits of flexibility and how to reap them. The second paradox reflects the differing attitudes of lower and higher management towards flexibility: top management determines where such flexibility will be implemented, whereas lower- and middle management must seek practices for implementing it and thus have a different perception than their superiors. The third paradox appears when management must identify relevant forms of flexibility and define optimal flexibility on a spectrum between total flexibility at a much higher cost and rigidity at minimal cost, without support for defining such optimality. Shukla et al. conclude that ignorance leads to paradoxical behaviour due to the limited availability of information on work practices, guidelines, operating procedures and strategies for effectively implementing flexibility.

A FLEXIBLE WORKPLACE ENABLES RESILIENT ACTIVITIES

Why are both organisational flexibility and individual autonomy needed in workplaces? What do they aim for, and how? In organisations, the immediate goal – if we forget the paradigmatic purpose of flexible capitalism – is to manage the uncertainty that arises from the risks, turbulences, obstacles, and challenges in the changing work environment to achieve resilience. Figure 2.2 shows the components of the adapting systems and the action regulation mechanism. People in organisations sense and anticipate the potential changes in the working environment, with their uncertainty, turbulences and risks, as challenges and opportunities, or as a mixture of these. They are distinguished by focusing on and diagnosing their critical features (left-hand column), which in turn are responded to by planning and deciding on the use of appropriate resources (right-hand column), including flexible work arrangements that influence the execution of an organisation's action strategy and, subsequently, its performance and employees' well-being.

Action Regulation in a Systemic Context

The model is based on four concepts from work and organisation psychology literature.

First, in the traditional *socio-technical systems (STS) theory*, work systems are considered open systems with respect to their external environment, continuously reorganising their internal sub-systems to achieve a steady state

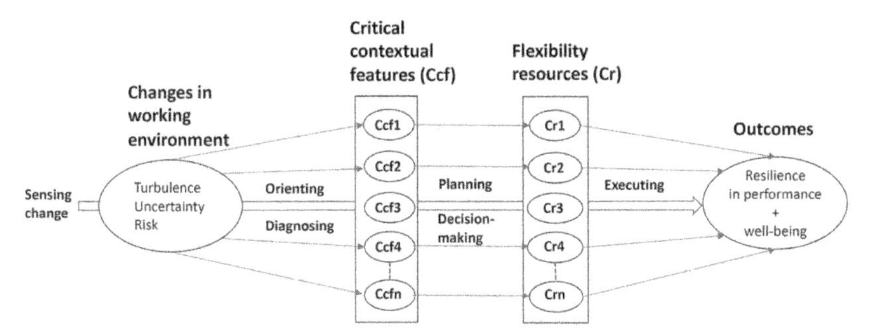

Figure 2.2 *Model for analysing the needs for flexibility, available resources and their outcomes*

at a level where they can still perform their tasks (Emery and Trist, 1997). This approach provides an opportunity to understand the relationship of an environment with actors on different levels, such as individuals, teams and organisations.

Second, *the fit theories*. The contingency theory on the organisational level refers to the idea that the best way to organise depends on the nature of the environment to which the organisation must relate (Scott, 1981). On the other hand, person–environment fit (P-E) theory refers to the compatibility or similarity between the person and the environment (Edwards, 2008). The fit theories emphasise that the demands placed on actors are relative to the capabilities and resources available to them to meet those demands. Later in this book, the job demands–resources (JD-R) model (Demerouti et al., 2001) is used as a fit framework to identify the demands and resources of hybrid work. In the JD-R model, job demands represent characteristics that potentially evoke strain and influence performance if they exceed the employee's adaptive resources (Bakker et al., 2007), that is, job and personal resources. For example, time flexibility may provide workers with resources for managing and responding to work and family demands.

Third, at the conceptual level, the model represents integrating the *resource-based views*. Again, these views are available both for organisations and individuals. Barney's (1991) view on organisational resources treatment is most concerned with understanding how resources contribute to competitive advantage; whereas the basic tenet of the conservation of resources theory (Hobfoll, 1988; Hobfoll et al., 2018) is that people strive to retain, protect and build resources, and that what is threatening to them is the potential or actual loss of these valued resources. For example, the missing interaction and contact with colleagues during the pandemic often created feelings of isolation, and sometimes deterioration of employee performance. This enforced the development of new organisational communication and leadership practices to verify fluent working processes. These two approaches to resources also underline the differences between the organisational and worker perspectives on flexibility.

The fourth element used in the model is *the action regulation theory* (Hacker, 2021). It provides frames to understand and describe how an individual or a team aims to autonomously and actively regulate their relationship and boundaries with their environments by orienting, diagnosing, planning, making decisions, and changing it by acting.

The Expected Outcomes

The recent turbulences experienced in working life and the world have raised discussions about developing *resilience* as the future critical capability and competence for individuals, teams, organisations and society. Flexible remote and teleworking arrangements, and using flexibility as a critical resource, could be crucial for developing such competency. This could be a springboard for scalable practices to navigate external disruptions such as pandemics in the future. Giustiniano et al. (2018, p. 3) define resilience as:

> Capacities to absorb external shocks and to learn from them while simultaneously preparing for and responding to external jolts, whether as organisations, teams or individuals. Resilience is claimed to be necessary to protect actors and agencies from shocks, crises, scandals, and business fiascos that generate fear and create dissonance. Resilient people and organisations get knocked down and get up again, ready to learn from events and to be ready for future challenges: The ultimate connotation of resilience.

Studies on team and organisational resilience vary considerably in their empirical context and disciplinary perspective. West et al. (2009, p. 253) suggest that team resilience allows teams to bounce back from failure, setbacks, conflicts and other threats which they may experience. Giustiniano et al. (2018) mention that resilience can manifest in two ways that complement each other: an adaptive response or a reactive response to external shocks and stressors. According to Duchek (2020, p. 215), organisational resilience can be conceptualised as a meta-capability, and inspired by process-based studies suggesting three successive resilience stages: anticipation, coping and adaptation. A fourth stage, of a formative innovative transformation, could be added to these three reactive stages. The transformation would mean an innovative and creative attitude, and actions that will shape work contexts and targets in a transformative manner.

The individual, team and organisational resiliencies are interdependent. Building resilience on the individual level can spread within an organisation and beyond, and collective cultural resilience can also make individuals more resilient. *Resilient individuals* can bounce back from stressful experiences quickly and efficiently, just as resilient metals bend but do not break (Fredrickson, 2001). Referring to psychological coping theory (Lazarus and Folkman, 1984), Fredrickson (2001, p. 222) suggests that positive emotions may fuel psychological resilience. Those studying organisational behaviour define resilience as the 'positive psychological capacity to rebound, to "bounce back" from adversity, uncertainty, conflict, failure, or even positive change, progress, and increased responsibility' (Luthans, 2002, p. 702). The Finnish concept of *Sisu* (Lahti, 2019) similarly refers to the ability of individuals to push through extreme challenges. As an attitude, individual resilience can be dated back to the teaching of the Stoics (Russell, 1945), that developing self-control, fortitude and calmness is the means to overcoming destructive emotions; in our case, related to turbulence at work.

NOTE

1. Flexible work, alternative work, work–life balance, family-friendly, work–family policies/balance, work–family conflict/family–work conflict, telework, flexitime, part-time work, telecommute, homework, remote work, compressed work/compressed hours, annualised hours, term-time working.

3. Hybrid work and its elements

A hybrid 'is something that is formed by combining two or more things'
(Merriam-Webster)

Hybrid work is a type of flexible work, in contrast to permanent, fixed work arrangements such as a regular eight-hour office working day, remote work and telework at home, and similar concepts. *Hybridity* is a designable characteristic of work systems and their components. In a study of the hybrid work definitions presented in the literature, and expectations during the pandemic (Vartiainen and Vanharanta, 2023), it was considered a flexible combination of various work elements. And the physical space element – work at the primary workplace and remote work in some other location – was the most common element characterising hybrid work, followed by the temporal element, that is, when, how long and how often work is done in each location and workplace. The social and virtual elements were used only occasionally to characterise hybrid work. The opportunities for setting goals and issues related to social interaction did not receive much attention. This chapter shows that hybrid work is more than the combination of two elements, and provides many more options to arrange working contexts and ways of action.

WHAT IS HYBRIDITY?

Many things, such as plants (a hybrid of two roses), vehicles (a hybrid car), and ethnicities (a Finnish-Congolese background), are made of 'two or more things'. In this book, the focus is only on hybrid work, organisations and workplaces. The basic concepts of hybridity, hybrid work, hybrid organisation and hybrid workplace are still evolving, leading to the following question: What are these 'two or more things' that justify using the term 'hybrid' in relation to work?

Typically, a systemic approach is used to identify a work system's basic, designable, functional and concrete elements. A work system acting in a working environment consists of an actor, its tools and the object of work. Identifying elements involves analysing the differences among different work systems, their environments and interactions. In practice this means, for example, comparing available hybrid work models in use. The essence of hybridity in each case is determined by the observer's understanding of the nature of the system and the ways it adapts to its environment, utilises its features and resources productively, and successfully develops work processes, including their creation. Work processes in an organisational context are goal- or purpose-driven and individually or collectively regulated. The systemic approach opens possibilities to discuss hybridity on the individual, team, organisation and societal levels, as these can all be seen as active work systems or actors in their respective environments. A hybrid workplace is systemic in that it consists of 'two or more things' that interplay with each other. As Besharov and Mitzinneck (2020, p. 3) argue, 'to achieve both analytical rigour and real-world relevance, research must account for variation in how hybridity is organisationally configured, temporally situated, and institutionally embedded'. Therefore, this chapter considers the concept of 'hybrid' from these different perspectives and levels.

Organisational Perspective

Discussions on *hybrid organisations* typically focus on the collaboration demands of networked organisations, and what a hybrid organisation must consider when implementing, organising and managing hybrid work from the perspectives of organisational performance and employee engagement. An example of a boundary-spanning hybrid organisation is a social–commercial hybrid (Radoynovska and Ruttan, 2021) consisting of non-profit, for-profit or born-hybrid organisations that combine social and commercial goals and identities to meet the needs of their common customers. Besharov and Mitzinneck (2020, p. 4) explain that when 'complex, intractable social problems continue to intensify, organisations increasingly respond with novel approaches that bridge multiple institutional spheres and combine forms, identities, and logics that would conventionally not go together', and organisational hybridity is created. Hybridity is needed and implemented when external hindrances and challenges need new actions and collaboration from diverse actors. Besharov and Mitzinneck also note that the configuration of organisational hybridity can vary, but also persist, evolving over time, and it both shapes and is shaped by the institutional environment. Hybrid organisations are heterogeneous. Besharov and Mitzinneck suggest that the configuration of organisational hybridity can vary along the following dimensions (ibid., pp. 5–8), which are applied here in a hybrid work context:

- The *compatibility* of a hybrid's constituent elements: to what extent do they entail consistent versus contradictory cognitions and actions? For example, information and communication technology (ICT) enables communication in a dispersed organisation, but simultaneously increases costs.

Compatibility can influence whether hybridity generates tensions between constituent elements or offers opportunities for synergy.

- *Centrality:* defined as the extent to which constituent elements are regarded as equally crucial, versus one element being dominant while others play a peripheral role. For example, time is critical in 'swift' or temporary teams as they must achieve their goals within a limited time. The goals are not achieved if other elements of a swift team, for example, working in different time zones, do not support scheduling.
- *Multiplicity:* or the number of constituent elements, which can bring together two or more conventionally distinct elements. More constituent elements may provide more choice and flexibility when making decisions or justifying proposed courses of action. On the other hand, more than two constituent elements can create instability and prove challenging to manage.
- *Structure:* as organisations may relatively flexibly combine and recombine integration and differentiation in the structures they develop. In integration, individuals and sub-groups, as well as organisational practices and divisions, combine and blend various elements of hybridity; whereas when differentiating, they carry out and enact just one element. The structure can affect the risk of conflict and mission drift in hybrid organisations.

Hybridity has also been discussed as a feature of more significant interaction and collaboration in a broader ecosystem consisting of cross-boundary interaction and collaboration among individuals and teams (Ancona et al., 2021). It is evident that blending different modes and working styles introduces practical complications in arranging working conditions and organising work in these spaces.

Hybrid teams as the basic unit of an organisation have been characterised over the years in many ways, but always as mixtures. It is common to compare them with co-located and virtual teams. However, it has been noticed that teams are diverse because many of their characteristics are variable. For example, Griffith and Neale (2001) made a difference between traditional, virtual and hybrid teams according to two dimensions of virtualness: (1) the time that team members spend together; and (2) the level of technology support they employ. In this case, hybrid teams are composed of members who interact over time, according to the moment's needs, through media and face-to-face contact determined by their adaptation and structuration of the work process (Figure 3.1). Fiol and O'Connor (2005) considered the relative absence of face-to-face contact to be one of the critical features of virtualness, because of its impact on group identification. Meeting in person is linked to a person's sense of belonging with a team – that is, group identification – and the extent of face-to-face contact among members is the most significant feature determining the effects of the other variables on identification processes (Fiol and O'Connor, 2005). Though a hybrid team may not be as virtual as a virtual team, its face-to-face contacts occasionally impact upon the quality of interaction. Since the pandemic, hybrid teams have been considered even more flexible. For example, Smite et al. (2023) defined hybrid teams based on fully flexible location and irregular presence in the office. Hybrid teams need not be completely virtual, yet different hybrid teams can occupy different ranges of the virtuality spectrum.

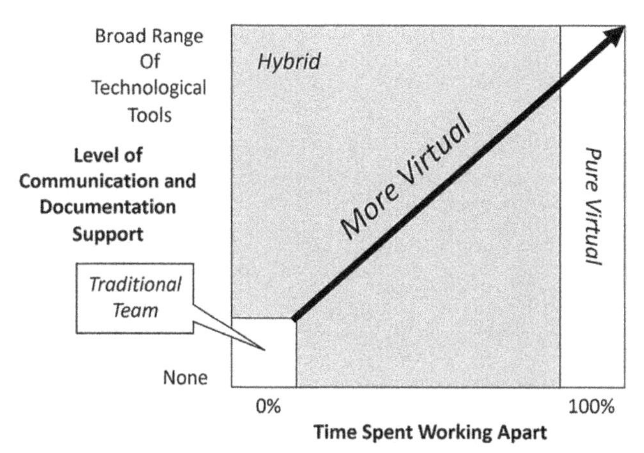

Source: Griffith and Neale (2001, p. 386).

Figure 3.1 *Hybrid team and the dimensions of virtualness*

Future Organisations

Some writers have outlined what post-pandemic work means for organisations and individuals. For example, Malhotra (2021) expects that knowledge work will increasingly be performed virtually, since switching to telework during the pandemic. The structure of organisations is expected to become more open, engaging external independent freelancers outside the organisation to work together on an ad hoc basis. An individual may work as part of multiple teams and on temporary projects. Therefore, individuals can and will have multiple reporting lines, and organisations will become more matrixed. For individuals, Malhotra highlights changes in locational, temporal and goal-related autonomy. However, according to him, the future of work will create challenges for organisations – and individuals – such as how to maintain organisational culture and identity, monitor performance, motivate dispersed employees, provide feedback for learning, enable work–life balance and foster social inclusion.

Recent developments have resulted in several new types of organisations and jobs: some hybrids of old elements, and some completely new. On the organisational level, there are an increasing number of 'all remote', dispersed organisations, meaning that employees are fully distributed, with every person working from a unique location (Rhymer, 2023). For example, Choudhury et al. (2020) describe the company GitLab, which does not have a physical office but employs 1000 people in more than 60 countries (Box 3.1).

BOX 3.1 CASE GITLAB

GitLab was incorporated in 2014 and operates in the software development tools industry. In September 2019, after its Series E round of funding, GitLab was valued at $2.7 billion.

GitLab is an 'all remote' company in that all 1000+ company employees located in 60+ different countries work remotely and typically asynchronously, often without ever meeting each other in the physical world. The organisation expanded significantly in 2019, from about 374 employees a year earlier.

GitLab develops tools that allow software engineers to automate many parts of the software development cycle, from initial planning to final deployment and monitoring of new code. It is widely recognised for its 'continuous integration' (CI) product, which enables teams of coders to slice a complex project into chunks, work in parallel on specialised tasks, and then combine the pieces into a functioning whole. Specifically, GitLab's CI tools automate the verification of the compatibility of newly contributed code to the existing code base. They thus represent the automation of the coordination work previously conducted by a human coder.

Apart from its 'all remote' model, GitLab is noteworthy to organisation designers for at least three other reasons. First, like many technology companies, it uses its own tools: GitLab (the company) uses GitLab (the product) to make improvements in GitLab (the product). Second, it also uses the same set of tools to organise and manage itself; for example, the company handbook, which exhaustively documents its formal organisational structure and processes, is developed, maintained and edited as if it were a code repository. Third, the handbook is public: anybody can view it inside or outside the company.

Source: Based on Choudhury et al. (2020, p. 2).

A common feature in *entirely virtual organisations* is the multi-purpose use of digital technologies, especially for communication, collaboration and the search for new knowledge. In his case study of six location-independent organisations, Rhymer (2023) describes many options to organise collaboration in these contexts. He identified two orientations to organise collaboration based on how employees interacted within each organisation: *a real-time orientation* and an *asynchronous orientation.* There were similarities, though. All organisations were interdependent and worked in teams to produce software products. All six organisations leveraged traditional hierarchies, with the number of layers correlated to their size. They worked in project cycles, typically four weeks, in stable, multidisciplinary teams, and conducted regular organisation-wide meetings (every 6–12 months). However, there were differences in practices. The asynchronous-oriented organisations had significantly fewer meetings each week. Also, responses to co-workers in those three organisations were left to the receiving employees' discretion, and no restrictions were placed on which hours of the day an individual could choose to work. Rhymer (2023) concludes that asynchronous-oriented organisations made intentional moves away from traditional patterns of interaction.

Another example of completely remote organisational configurations is working on online and offline platforms, where freelancers often globally implement client assignments. Although the number of platform workers is still low, it is growing, mainly due to the COVID-19 pandemic (ILO, 2021b). For example, the Online Labour Index (OLI) produced by Kässi and Lehdonvirta (2018; see also Kässi et al., 2021) showed that in May 2021, the number of projects started on platforms had increased by 93 per cent from May 2016.

HYBRIDISING MECHANISM

A hybrid work system is seldom stable and permanent, therefore becoming and being a hybrid unit is a time-bound process. It is expected that the configuration of basic elements changes over time. When a hybrid work unit, for example a team, is seen as a work system within a larger environment, its specific mandate, structure, form and work process itself, with its outcomes, are determined mainly by three intertwined and partly embedded factors: the purpose of the work, the hindering or enabling features of its context, and the available resources (Hacker, 2021). These factors hinder or/and facilitate the unit's fluent work process and its regulation (Figure 3.2). The purpose of work and the tasks are defined as the main driving force in initiating the work process by an individual, a team or an organisation. For example, the assignment of a team within an organisation may be determined based on the intra-organisational division of labour. In turn, the team redefines that mandate by dividing it into tasks assigned to each team member and artificial intelligence (AI)-supported tools.

The *common goals* characterise the purpose of an organisation, and they are expected to generate the personnel's joint efforts and commitment to their achievement. Usually, the objectives are set by the organisation's management, with or without consulting employees, and are related to productivity and economic outcomes. The organisation's values, such as sustainability, often justify profit expectations. On the individual and team levels, the organisational objectives affect the complexity of individual and collective assignments and tasks; that is, whether routine or creative task execution is required in the work. Bell and Kozlowski (2002) claimed that task complexity has critical implications for the structure and processes of teams. They are created to handle various tasks ranging from the simple (for example, command and control) to the complex (for example, brainstorming). Analogously, the content of tasks influences the structure and workflow of the hybrid work unit and what kinds of resources are needed to regulate work activities. Besides the common goals, the expectations of fulfilling the basic individual needs drive the hybridisation process.

The *contextual demands* and their features may hinder or challenge achieving an organisation's objectives. They can also provide benefits and opportunities that support and help in the hybrid transformation. Their identification enables the design of features of a work unit and what resources are required from both the organisation and workers.

Purpose and context influence what kinds of internal and external *resources* individuals or collective subjects, such as a team, need to regulate work processes, relations and boundaries among subjects, the relevant objects and tasks, and the environment and influence what outcomes are possible.

The configuration elements provide the options to design and build different hybrid work units.

The *outcomes* of an individually or collectively regulated work process can be used as evaluation criteria showing the success of activities, the functionality and quality of performance outcomes, and their effects on employees' well-being and commitment. These criteria can also inform the values in planning and developing hybrid work, and the best fit between demands and resources.

Next, the contextual demands and enabling resources are explored and described as workspace elements.

WORKSPACE ELEMENTS IN FLEXIBLE HYBRID WORK

The workspace concept returns to the field theory of Lewin (1972) and the 'Ba' concept of Nonaka et al. (2000). Lewin introduced the idea that everyone

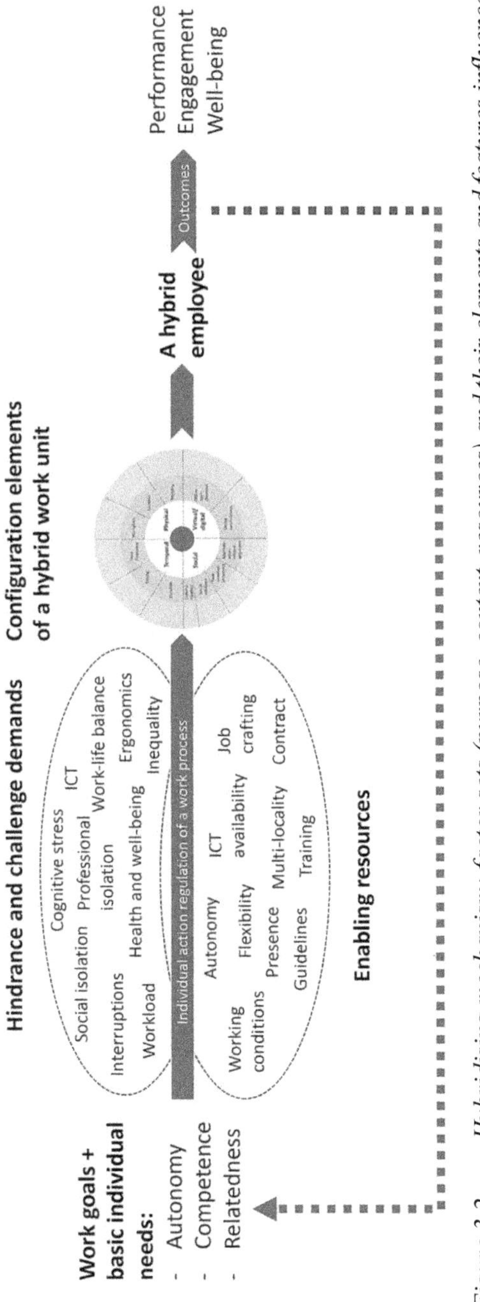

Figure 3.2 *Hybridising mechanism: factor sets (purpose, context, resources) and their elements and features influence the configuration of individual hybrid work and its potential outcomes*

exists in a psychological force field called the 'life space' determining and limiting a person's behaviour. *Life space* is a highly subjective environment that characterises the world as the individual sees it, while remaining embedded in the objective elements of physical and social fields. 'Mental space', the concept used in this book, is equivalent to the 'life space' as the experienced state of an individual. In the mental space, an individual regulates their activities with their mind. According to Lewin (1951), behaviour (*B*) is the function (*f*) of a person (*P*) and their environment (*E*), $B = f(P, E)$. Similarly, individuals, teams and organisations as actors are in active interaction with their environments and working contexts.

Nonaka et al. (2000) further enlarged the life space concept with their concept of 'Ba'. It refers to a shared context in which knowledge is shared, created and utilised by those who interact and communicate there. Ba does not just refer to a physical space, but also to a specific time and space that integrates layers of spaces. Ba unifies the physical space (such as an office space), virtual space (such as email), the social space (such as colleagues), and the mental space (such as individual or everyday experiences, ideas and ideals shared by people with common goals in a working context). For individuals or groups, modern work contexts are combinations of physical, virtual, social and temporary working spaces that change over time. Because of the strong influence of time, the term 'temporal space' is used to describe how other spaces tend to change in time.

The needs and properties of self-regulation in the human mind can be specified based on the workspace concepts. *Mental space* reflects the perceptions and experiences of individuals as the outcomes of the space elements' integration. The human mind, in the meaning 'I will do' or collectively 'We will do', guides and controls behavioural actions in these spaces. Later in this chapter, the term 'mental space' is used to denote a cognitive-emotional platform resourcing the human mind guiding action regulation processes. Parts of psychological processes are conscious, and parts unconscious, based on the learning and routinisation of some mental operations and actions.

Next, the four basic physical, virtual, social and temporal elements impacting an individual's perceived life space or mental space are described in more detail. The four elements are used for constructing the preliminary hybrid work model. Chapter 4 uses the model to analyse the content of hybrid work definitions in the literature. Each basic element has its sub-elements, and a sub-element includes designable and adjustable features such as working at home, using online technologies, communicating face-to-face, and working fixed days at the office each week. For example, some hybrid work definitions use workplaces as the defining characteristic of hybrid work. In these definitions, the physical element is referred to as: 'working in [the] office and [at] home', 'not [a] dedicated workplace in [the] office', and 'working elsewhere'. Others definitions often refer to time, for example: 'two home days', 'three office days' and 'occasional telecommuting'. The preliminary model is complemented in the coming chapters with additional features to implement, develop and manage hybrid work units.

Physical Space

It is beneficial to differentiate between *workplace* and *location* as sub-elements of physical space. They are related conceptually and in practice, as workplaces located somewhere are physical spaces or places of employment where someone works for their employer or themselves. The workplace and its location are spatial elements to be planned; they materialise, for example, as a desk in an open office space or as a private room, and can include working mainly in the office or elsewhere. A physical space turns into a workplace when used for work as its physical setting. The availability of workplaces in different locations and the opportunity to choose which workplaces to use are powerful enablers of hybrid work (Vartiainen et al., 2007).

Mobility is a sub-element of determinable physical spaces because a person can move both within and between workplaces, to benefit from the variety of locations and workplaces available. In addition, moving from one location to another always happens in some materialised context, usually in a vehicle, which can also be used as a working and living environment. Moving regularly within and between different locations is called multi-mobility, and continually moving among different sites is called full or total mobility. Lilischkis (2003) used a still-valid topology based on the dimensions of physical and temporal spaces to identify physically mobile employees. Physical space criteria include: (1) the number of locations; (2) the similarity among locations; (3) whether there is a default workplace to return to; (4) whether work takes place while moving or at a destination; (5) whether work can take place at fixed locations without changing between them; (6) whether there are limitations in the work area; and (7) the distance between locations. Time criteria include: (1) the frequency of location changes; (2) the time spent moving among work locations; and (3) the time spent at a specific work location if not moving. Types of mobile workers each have their basic physical space and time criteria. 'On-site movers' work in a limited work area, 'yo-yos' return to a main office, 'pendulums' have two recurrent work locations, 'nomads' work in more than two places, and 'carriers' cannot do their work at a fixed location and must work while moving.

The more locations and workplaces there are to visit, and the more distant they are from each other, the higher the pressure felt from work demands to regulate work processes. The features of both location and workplace as spatial elements are *multilinearly interdependent*. As shown in Figure 3.3, the distance between workplaces increases the need for physical mobility if a teleworker wants to meet a colleague or customer in person. The need for a physical meeting can be eliminated by using collaboration technologies if the task permits it. An actor's contextual complexity also increases when there are several locations to visit, and when the location changes, often because the physical working conditions, digital infrastructure and people are different in each location. Challenges also arise in the design and development of the organisation. How should work be coordinated when people are working in different locations? What new competencies do employees and management need? What are the ergonomic and working conditions to enable work in each place? The relationships of such features are quite sensitive and fluid, and their balance is thus precarious. If a group and its members are physically mobile, this affects other work features. Mobility means more locations at which work takes place, more people to meet, and a greater need to coordinate joint actions. The combination of spatial elements may determine, for example, whether a team is temporary and fluid.

Potential *workplace locations* in hybrid work include (Vartiainen, 2007, p. 29): (1) the employee's home; (2) the main workplace (the employer's premises); (3) vehicles, such as cars, buses, trams, trains, planes and ships; (4) a customer's or partner's premises, or an alternative premises of the company ('other workplaces'); and (5) hotels, cafés, parks, and so on ('third workplaces'). Oldenburg (1989), for example, listed cafés, coffee shops, community centres, general stores, bars and other meeting places as 'third workplaces'. Third places are conceptualised as physical spaces that are easily accessible for people to enjoy each other's company outside of home and work. Online and virtual environments can serve as 'digital third places' (Parkinson et al., 2022). Critical questions about hybrid work in such locations are how these places differ as working contexts or workplaces, what places are used in practice, and how such places should be physically and virtually equipped.

In discussions on post-pandemic workplaces, *physical arrangements* have dominated the discussion, including how employees can be attracted back to the office and what kinds of offices there should be. For example, Kane et al. (2021) suggest that physical workplaces should enable flexibility by, for example, providing spaces appropriate for a group to brainstorm, host a workshop or conduct daily meetings. Holtham (2008, p. 455) lists seven core affordances that an office should offer: it should function as: (1) a formal meeting place for colleagues and business associates; (2) a base for mobile and remote workers; (3) a base for static workers; (4) a base for information-intensive work processes; (5) a base for knowledge-intensive work processes; (6) a space that provides opportunities for serendipitous human-to-human contact, hence stimulating creativity and innovation; and (7) a symbol of the organisation to both external and internal audiences. At the same time, employee

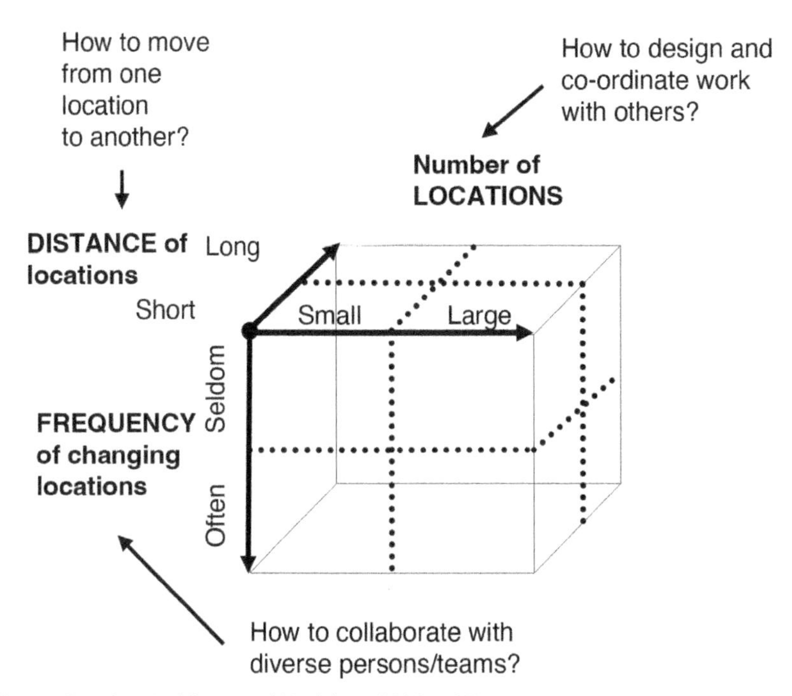

Source: Based on Andriessen and Vartiainen (2006, p. 37).

Figure 3.3 An example of the interdependence of the features of the location sub-element and work-related challenges

preferences should be considered; for example, a preference for a dedicated desk in the workplace.

Other locations can and should be evaluated similarly based on their physical affordances. However, a question arises: What kinds of *features* should each workplace in the organisation have to enable smooth working? Blomberg and Kallio (2022), in their recent review of the physical context of creativity, suggest using McCoy's (2005) five spatial elements, which are also related to social dynamics and behaviour in each workplace. The spatial organisation defines the spatial aspects of the work environment, such as the size, shape, arrangement and division of space. These features can affect privacy, control, flexibility, and so on. Architectonic details include fixed or stationary aesthetics and materials or ornaments such as decorative styles, signs, colours and artwork. These features may be necessary from the standpoint of a group's identity. Office or work station views include what can be seen from windows and adjacent workspaces. These views can contain either relaxing or stressful elements. Workplace resources for employees, such as access to equipment, parking and food services, and ambient conditions, including heating, illumination, ventilation, and acoustics, are essential aspects of the work environment.

In addition to increased autonomy in decision-making, the content of tasks and jobs impact workplace functionality: work requiring deep focus is more accessible in a silent place at home or a private room at an office, whereas face-to-face interaction with others during lunchtime is easier at an office. However, the quality of working conditions in the workplace is even more important than the location itself, be it the main workplace, the home or any other place, as good working conditions facilitate work completion. During the pandemic, homes have been converted into workplaces in various ways, depending greatly on, for example, the size of the space available and the technologies in use. At the same time, workspaces in the main offices have often been empty.

Virtual Space

A 'virtual space' refers to the global Internet, online platforms, and an organisation-wide intranet as a workplace for the digital labourer and a collaborative working environment (CWE) for members of dispersed teams. A *virtual workplace* is such a place in a virtual space that is used for work and collaboration. Complex virtual spaces integrate many communication tools, such as email, audio and videoconferencing, group calendar, chat, document management and presence awareness tools, into a collaborative working environment, such as a three-dimensional (3D) virtual environment, that is, a virtual world.

Halford (2005) related her concept of the 'hybrid workspace' to developing information and communication technologies that enable remote working outside organisational settings, usually from home in addition to other places without face-to-face contact. According to her:

> There is a hollowing out of the fixed organisational workspace and a polarisation towards the relocation of work into domestic space on the one hand and the dislocation of work into cyberspace on the other … These individuals work at home and engage in embodied organisational spaces; they conduct relationships virtually and in close proximity. How does this combination of organisational and domestic spaces, mediated in cyberspace, impact on practices of work, organisation and management? (ibid., pp. 19–20)

In her study, Halford shows that spatial hybridity changes the nature of work, organisation and management in domestic space, cyberspace and organisational space. It can be said that spatial hybridity results from combining physical, virtual or digital spaces with social spaces in use; spaces put into use for work then turn into workplaces in concrete terms.

In this early definition, the *differentia specifica* of hybridity and its elements are place or location (for example, home, other places) as a physical space, and cyberspace as virtual or digital space for both doing solo work and interacting with others in a social space, that is, enabling collaboration. This definition is closely related to the concept of a blended workplace as, for example, described by Tredinnick and Laybats (2021, p. 108): 'Blended work combines the advantages of physical and virtual work environments, allowing hybrid modes of work where individuals dip in and out of virtual and physical spaces.'

The role of virtual spaces as workplaces has grown as mobile information and communication technologies increasingly enable flexible working from multiple physical locations. A whole class of digital labourers has emerged worldwide, working for international employers (Scholz, 2013) and often doing micro-tasks as freelancers. Locally, in organisations, many knowledgeable workers 'escape' from their main office to their homes or public places where they can do their jobs, concentrating in peace. A virtual space enables them to access knowledge and their clients, and collaborate with colleagues.

An important feature of virtual space is that its tools enable organisation members to work alone and together *offline* (asynchronously) and *online* (synchronously) when employees are physically dispersed across multiple locations. The pandemic forced many to telework from home and learn to use digital technologies for the first time, as communication tools and collaboration platforms became necessary. New tools and applications were used; for example, online meetings became routine, and many restaurants adopted virtual ordering and delivery services.

In the future, the development and growth of telework and remote and digital online work will be tightly integrated with the development of technologies, expanding 5G bandwidths and emerging 6G bandwidths, AI applications and ever-smarter mobile devices. Through broadband mobile Internet and digital labour platforms, there is access to multiple communication functions, including email, the Internet, instant messaging, text messaging and company networks. It is evident that digitalisation changes the working environment; impacts working processes, tasks and job content; and affects structures and organisations, products and services in many ways, resulting in the need for new competencies, organisation and ways of working (Schaffers et al., 2020). Some future expectations concerning virtual space are discussed in Chapter 9.

Social Space

A social space is one of the defining elements in hybrid work, as individual solo work is more an exception than a rule. Social space covers *communication* and social interaction in physical and virtual settings. For example, *social support*, such as advice and help, can come from various sources, including co-workers, supervisors, customers, family and friends (Taylor, 2011). People may have the option to work in solitude, doing remote work alone or in person with others, online or offline, asynchronously or synchronously, and at the main workplace or any other location.

Figure 3.4 provides an example of an individual's work events for one day. A working day starts at home alone by reading and responding to emails asynchronously. After a bus ride to the main workplace, preparations for an online meeting start there. Discussions with colleagues at the office are face-to-face during lunch and in two previously arranged meetings. Then comes a period of messaging with distant team members, and finally, the working day ends in two minor face-to-face meetings before the worker returns home. Hybridity consists of working remotely at home, virtually and asynchronously with others, and synchronously with others at the main workplace. A work day for a hybrid worker is a mixture of working in different spaces.

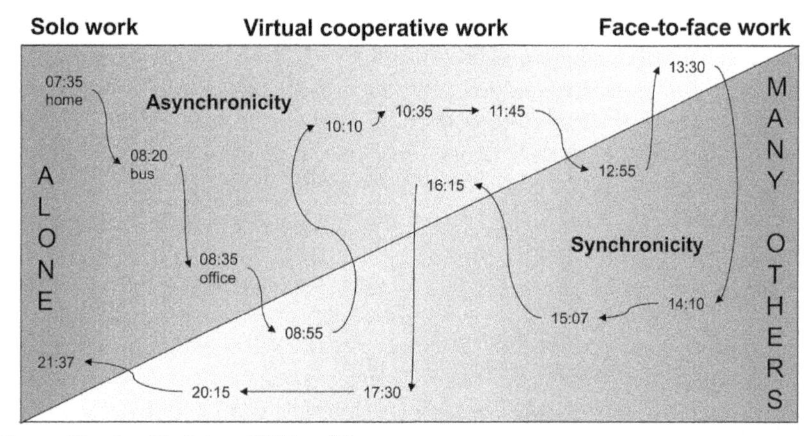

Source: Based on Vartiainen (2007, p. 50).

Figure 3.4 *A mobile multilocational worker's work day is a mixture of working alone, asynchronously and synchronously with others*

Communication is a critical and necessary enabler of social interaction and collaboration in hybrid work. The basic *types of interaction* in collaborative efforts – that is, task- and group-oriented processes – are based on communication among individuals (e.g., Andriessen, 2003, pp. 144–145) and between human actors and AI tools. *Task-oriented processes* in interactions include information sharing and mutual learning, cooperation, and coordination processes between interaction participants. Information is shared by providing and developing information and knowledge. Cooperation refers to working together in practice; for example, designing a concept, product or service together. Coordination is needed to adjust each group member's work to the work of others and the goal of the whole group. For example, simple tasks require less coordination, and their competence requirements are lower than in the case of complex tasks. *Group maintenance-oriented processes* or social interaction refer to team-building for developing trust and cohesion. Factors that enable hybrid work at the team level should support these processes. The main criterion when selecting collaboration technologies is the complexity of communication and collaboration tasks. To navigate such complexity, various available adaptation mechanisms include, for example, providing recruitment or training, or changing the tasks, context or tools used.

In the hybrid work context, the flexible use of places generates variance in face-to-face social contact; for example, with one's family at home and colleagues at the main workplace. Separating solo work from collaborative work is often challenging, even when physically isolated at home. In this type of *'pseudoprivacy'* (Becker and Sims, 2000, p. 15), emails, text messages, calls and online virtual meetings often interrupt work. Thus, the nature of work requires presence at several levels, creating a need to be 'multipresent'. This *'multipresence'* (Koroma and Vartiainen, 2018) is mobile workers' urge to be simultaneously present in physical, virtual and social spaces while working across boundaries from multiple locations and on the move. States of presence arise from different combinations of physical, virtual and social spaces, ranging from absence to presence, both socially and virtually. However, this increasing findability and awareness of other people's locations and availability on the Internet can reduce the feeling of autonomy and increase that of external control, resulting in a paradoxical situation. Leonardi et al. (2010) called this the *'connectivity paradox'*, as teleworkers sometimes use their advanced ICTs strategically to decrease, rather than increase, the distance they feel from colleagues.

Temporal Space

In addition to the flexible use of physical, virtual and social spaces, the essential factor in hybrid work is the flexibility of time. The temporal element has three sub-elements: duration, timing and frequency. *'Duration'* concerns how long something happens in units of time, that is, minutes, hours, days, weeks, months or years. For example, a hybrid employee may be allowed to work two weeks per month remotely or work four weeks abroad. *'Timing'* refers to when something is done or comes about, whether something happens during certain hours of the day or certain days in a week. For example, a hybrid employee may work on the employer's premises the whole day on Monday and Friday. *'Time frequency'* is how often something happens during a period, whether something happens every hour, daily, weekly, monthly or constantly, and whether it happens regularly or occasionally. For example, a hybrid employee may occasionally work at home.

In knowledge work, the use of digital tools allows collaborating employees to operate around the clock and enables individuals to complete their portion of the work at any time. Collaboration is needed across countries and time zones in more complex situations. The temporal element also has other features that impact upon the configuration of a hybrid work unit. Temporariness is one such feature, dictating the formation of new work units for one-time projects, the time individuals can disconnect, and what work schedules will be followed; for example, time allocations for individuals vary because of participating in multiple projects. One critical issue in hybrid work is who – the employer, the employee, or both together – is authorised to decide what days in a week or weeks in a month are teleworking days/weeks, or the daily hours for teleworking.

Time is also critical because hybrid work, contextual demands and available resources can change continuously. The work environment is expected to *change over time* – sometimes slowly, but also unexpectedly – pressing an individual to adapt and an organisation to change. An example of an unexpected external reason experienced across the globe was the COVID-19 pandemic that began in early 2020. It forced millions to shift swiftly to remote work and telework from home. However, other minor reasons can initiate change; for example, changes in service and product demand. The reasons for change are multiple; they are often external but can also be internal, such as missing expertise in an organisation.

The change reflects the needed configuration of the basic elements, sub-elements, and features (Figures 3.5a and 3.5b). The figures illustrate how using multiple locations, working primarily alone, and using digital tools to access data sources, change during a given period; working both in the office and at home, daily with others, and through virtual collaboration. It illustrates how fragile the hybrid work arrangement can be, due to its dependency on what is done and where.

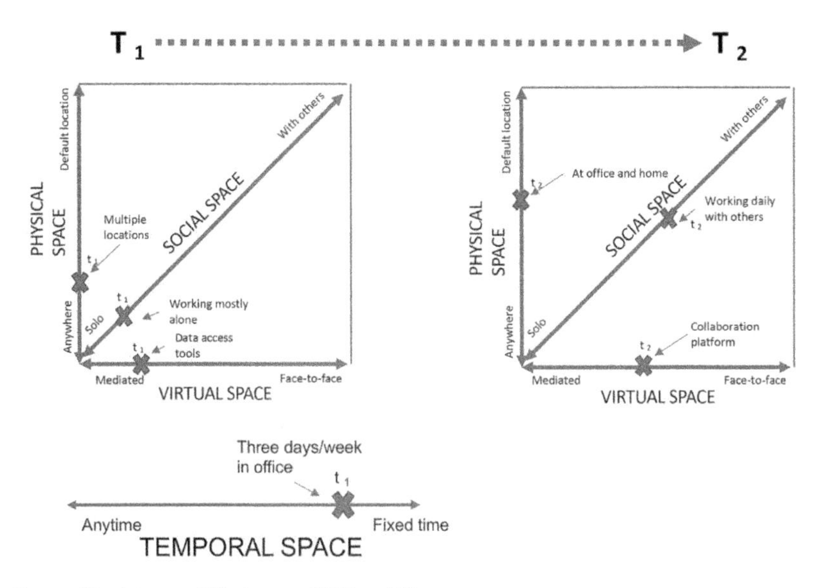

Source: Vartiainen and Vanharanta (2023, p. 71).

Figure 3.5a Using the basic elements, sub-elements and features depends on time and contextual demands

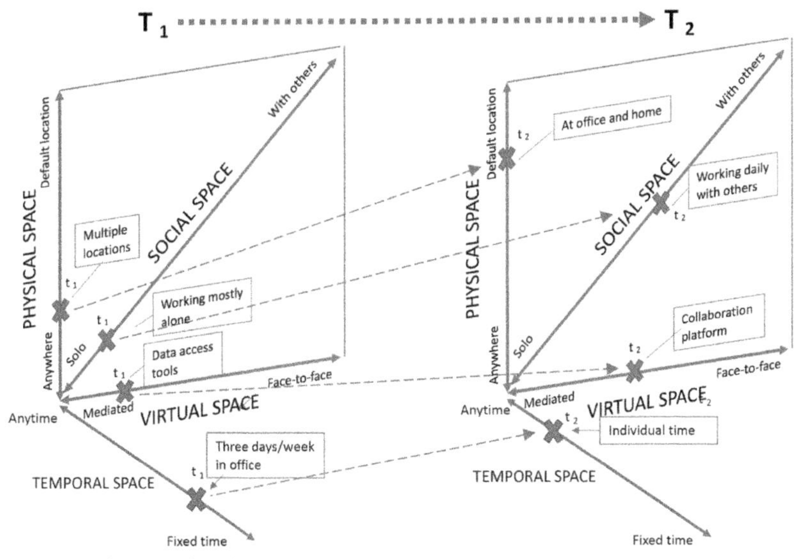

Source: Vartiainen and Vanharanta (2023, p. 71).

Figure 3.5b Changing goals and contexts bring dynamism to hybrid work

Physical and Temporal Spaces

The spaces are interrelated, as they exist in all hybrid work units. The *interdependence of time and place* illustrates this. For example, Gratton (2021) describes the interplay of workplace and time from the viewpoint of their flexible use. Before the COVID-19 pandemic, physical space and time were limited, because most employees were expected to work in the office for a specific period. At the beginning of the pandemic, there was a sudden working shift from place-constrained (in the office) to place-unconstrained (working anywhere, though mainly at home). Simultaneously, there was a shift in time use, going from time-constrained (working synchronously with others) to time-unconstrained (working asynchronously whenever the worker chose). The interplay of the physical and temporal spaces – and other spaces – creates the potential to realise hybrid work in many ways depending on how much flexibility is possible and allowed (Figure 3.6).

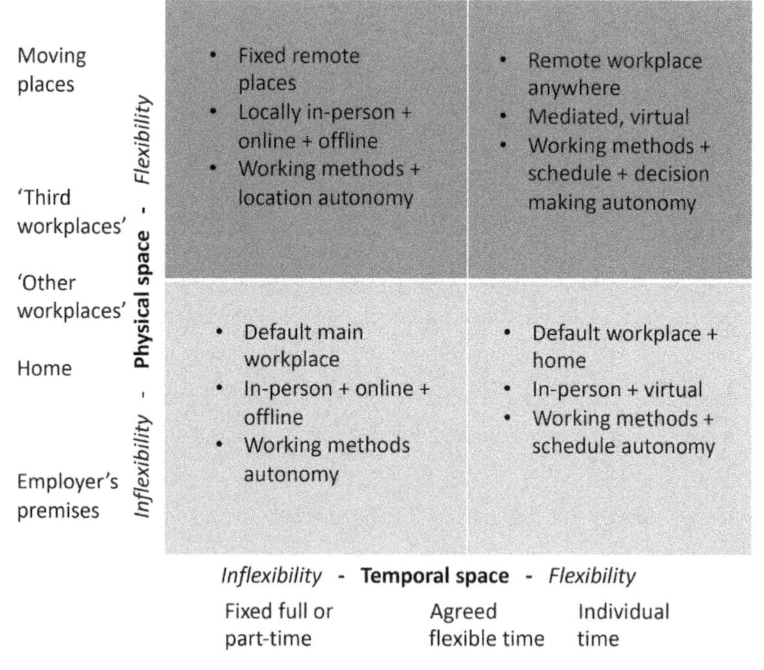

Figure 3.6 Work arrangements in terms of location and time

It is also important to note that both the duration and timing of workplace use vary, which impacts upon how these elements are managed. The demands of the business and the needs of the individuals change over time. This increases the fluidity and transiency of the mixture of hybrid work elements needed.

The interplay of physical, social and virtual elements in hybrid work is shown, for example, when creativity and innovativeness are needed in each job. During the aftermath of the pandemic, some companies have been worried about the repercussions of forced working from home on innovation and innovativeness. For example, Arena et al. (2022) warn that there is now a long-term threat to the ability of organisations to innovate. According to them, research shows that face-to-face interactions in teams are critical to innovation, because they often develop and persist through casual micro-interactions during lunchtime and similar ad hoc interactions in the workplace. Drawing on social network theory, they show how each of the three stages of innovation (idea generation, idea incubation and scaling) can be undermined by virtual work. They propose an alternative organisational design that leaders can adopt to overcome these limitations: the adaptive hybrid model. The model builds on a blend of intentionally virtual and face-to-face work to avoid the loss of social connections, and suggests diverse types of connections for each of the three stages of innovation. The model is adaptive and flexible, as employees must be in the office for the 'moments that matter'.

MENTAL SPACE

Vygotsky believed that human consciousness was developed only through mediated action in cultural, historical, and institutional settings (cited in Hasan and Kazlauskas, 2014). Hence, he proposed building the connection between an individual and the environment by modelling the mediated action. The subject, the object and the mediating artefact/tool form the mediated action triangle. The *'mental space'* refers to the cognitive-emotional structure and processes of the human mind. Information and knowledge from the working environment are collected and reflected in mental space, interpreted as cognitions and affective states, and used to regulate work activities (Figure 3.7). The space elements, sub-elements, and their features impact upon how the work is experienced in organisations. The action regulation itself happens on different levels. Parts of these psychological processes are conscious, and parts are unconscious, based on the learning and routinisation of some mental operations and actions. The outcomes are shown in the well-being and performance of individuals, teams and organisations. These outcomes can be used as the evaluation criteria to design, redesign and develop work and job crafting that focus on the rearrangements of the physical, virtual, social and temporal space elements.

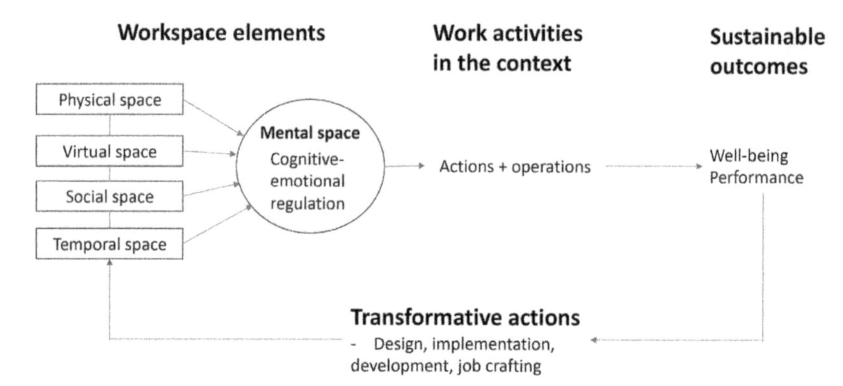

Figure 3.7 *The cyclical relationship of the basic space elements to the mental space, action regulation, potential outcomes and transformative actions*

As an example of the experienced states, the *paradoxes of flexible work* are reflected in the state of mind and mood. As discussed in Chapter 2, the autonomy paradox (Mazmanian et al., 2013) or flexibility paradox (Chung, 2022) appears on the individual level when an autonomous and self-managing employee works voluntarily all the time and everywhere, often with negative impacts on work–life balance, well-being and health. Paradoxes can also be interpreted as tensions in the mental space as the outcomes of contradictions in the work system and its environment. Building on cultural-historical activity theory, Engeström et al. (2022) analysed school children's experiences in six worlds: family, school, peers, digital, civic and future activity. Children experienced their worlds as mutually penetrating hybridised configurations. Hybridisation was a source of tensions ranging from dilemmas to conflicts, critical conflicts and double binds. They were seen in all six worlds. The world of school was the most highly hybridised, and the most hybridised was the relationship between school and peer activity. Similarly, in organisations, the physical space does not necessarily support interaction and possible personal meetings, or the available technologies may lack some tools for versatile communication. In Chapters 5 and 6 of this book, the potential outcomes of space element arrangements are described in terms of the hindrances and challenges of job demands, and their benefits and opportunities.

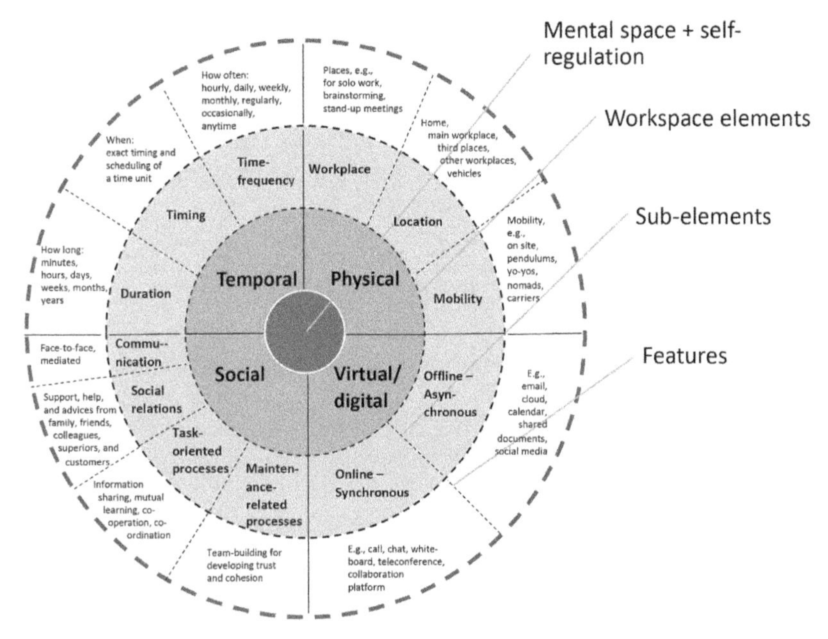

Source: Vartiainen and Vanharanta (2023, p. 25).

Figure 3.8 The preliminary model of hybrid work: adjustable basic elements, their sub-elements, and some features

THE PRELIMINARY FLEXIBLE HYBRID WORK MODEL

The preliminary basic elements of hybrid work are physical, virtual/digital, social and temporal workspaces. These elements are interconnected, each with designable and actionable properties, that is, features. They impact upon the contents of the mental space (Figure 3.8). How these elements interplay and intersect depends on the concrete needs of work arrangements, that is, hybridising mechanisms described above. Affordances, that is, the action potential of the basic and sub-elements, are evident in their features. These features are designable, customisable, interchangeable and, most importantly, adaptively combinable.

The concepts of hybrid work and workspaces embody the flexibility paradigm, balancing varying individual needs with organisations' performance goals. A hybrid entity combines two or more elements flexibly to provide resilience in changing, unstable, turbulent environments and situations. *The purpose, working context and regulation of a work process and the expected outcomes impact upon what features of an organisation's practice will be combined for hybrid work.* These constituent building blocks of hybrid work can be used by workplace design specialists and personnel crafting their jobs when designing and changing work. 'Job crafting' refers to proactive behaviour where employees customise their job demands and resources (Tims et al., 2012), and adjust their working practice and work environment to suit their tasks and individual preferences. This also applies to team-level job crafting, where team members restructure their work.

Next, the affordances of basic elements, sub-elements, and their features of hybrid work are summarised.

Location, workplace and mobility and their features are the sub-elements of the physical space. Work can be done in various workplaces in different neighbourhoods, urban and rural areas, different parts of the same country, multiple countries and globally. The workplaces in each location vary in terms of physical premises and working contexts according to an organisation's and its employees' needs. Mobility brings about a contextual change in locations and workplaces.

The virtual space enables *online and offline* work by affording various digital tools and software to seek information and knowledge, produce products and services, and communicate and collaborate synchronously and asynchronously with others or work alone.

The social space includes sub-elements to guarantee fluent face-to-face or mediated *communication* processes, maintaining *social relationships* and *task-related* awareness, and *team processes*.

The temporal space includes time-related features that help to determine *when, for how long and how often* work is done. For example, 'timing' refers to determining when something is done or comes about; for example, whether one works at the office every Friday afternoon, or whenever and wherever one wants to. 'Duration' refers to decisions on how long something exists or lasts; for example, whether one works at the office for a full day or only part of a day. 'Time frequency' refers to how often something happens within a unit of time; for example, whether one works at home twice a week or every day. A hybrid work system emerges in a new type of space that flexibly merges physical, virtual, social, and temporal elements and sub-elements with their features.

The mental space integrates the impacts of the contextual elements as *individual experiences* that are used to regulate activities through individual mindset. How these elements and their features should be organised and combined in each concrete hybrid work arrangement depends on the job content and the expected psychological and organisational outcomes. These issues are addressed in the following chapters. In addition, the preliminary hybrid work model is further developed.

It is suggested that the hybrid work model is adaptive. In an organisation, its goals, and tasks to be done strategically, determine who is needed to be where and when, and what kind of collaboration is needed. The superior, or in agreement with the employee or team, directs the employees to be present in person or virtually as dictated by the task, work environment, and personal and social resources. For example, in innovation tasks, more time is needed for in-person meetings than for a routine knowledge service task. The preliminary hybrid work model emphasises using flexible ways of the appropriate set of social network connections.

4. Towards flexible hybrid work

The COVID-19 pandemic was a disruptor and provided a quasi-experimental setting to study worldwide the implementation and outcomes of remote and telework, mostly from home, among those who were teleworking for the first time. During the first two years, a lively discussion started about experiences concerning work from home (WFH) and the post-pandemic future and working life. This chapter discusses hybrid work and how it was experienced and defined during the pandemic.

The preliminary model of hybrid work was used as the frame to analyse the discussion in literature published during the pandemic, in addition to European data collected from 27 European countries in early 2022 (Vartiainen and Vanharanta, 2023).[1] During the early phases of the pandemic in 2020–2022, hybrid work concepts started to emerge in business journals and the reports of consulting and other companies. A sample of such works was collected to determine how to define hybrid work.

The articles were read, paragraphs mentioning the definition of hybrid work were searched, and the content was analysed and described in terms of the basic elements and sub-elements of hybrid work and their features.

PROFESSIONAL EXPECTATIONS CONCERNING HYBRID WORK

The resulting comparison shows that the physical space element was commonly used in the definitions of hybrid work as using a flexible mixture of locations, working both on the employer's premises and remotely elsewhere (Table 4.1). In addition, the temporal element was used, that is, to indicate when, how often and for how long hybrid work is employed. Social and virtual spaces were seldom mentioned. However, other characterisations, such as flexibility, agility and the use of autonomy by both employers and employees, were mentioned. These features were potential new ingredients to the preliminary hybrid work concept beyond physical and virtual spaces, time and social elements.

Table 4.1 *Examples of hybrid work definitions by consulting companies, business journals and international organisations during the pandemic*

SOURCE	DEFINITION: hybrid work, a hybrid worker	ELEMENTS	SUB-ELEMENTS, FEATURES
Consulting company publications			
Capgemini 2020, The future of work: From remote to hybrid, (Crummenerl et al., 2020)	'A hybrid workforce essentially refers to a workforce that is distributed across different locations, from traditional office and factory spaces to remote locations, including within employees' living space, be it a family home or shared apartment. A hybrid working model is characterized by the flexibility and choices it offers employees, and it can be an innovative way of driving new approaches to agility, collaboration, and ways of working.'	Physical space Social space	Main workplace, multiple locations, home, social relations, flexibility, autonomy
BCG 2021, Decoding Global Ways of Working, March 2021, (Strack et al., 2021)	'It is indeed flexibility that most people are interested in, not a 180-degree turn in the traditional model that would have everyone working from home all the time and never going to a physical work location.'	Physical space	Home, main workplace, flexibility
McKinsey & Company 2021 (Alexander et al., 2021)	'As the pandemic eases, executives say that the hybrid model – in which employees work both remotely and, in the office – will become far more common.'	Physical space	Main workplace, multiple locations
Microsoft New Future of Work Report 2022 (Teevan et al., 2022)	'For individuals, hybrid work refers to working part of the time in the office and part time from somewhere else. For organizations, hybrid can also refer to having a mix of fully on-site and fully off-site employees.'	Physical space Temporal space Social space	Multiple locations, duration, face-to-face
Gallup, The Future of Hybrid Work March 15, 2022 (Wigert, 2022)	'Employees with the ability to work remotely are largely anticipating a hybrid office environment going forward – one that allows them to spend part of their week working remotely and part in the office.'	Physical space Temporal space	Multiple locations, duration
Business journals			
Harvard Business Review (e.g., Gratton, 2021)	'To design hybrid work properly, you have to think about it along two axes: place and time … an anywhere, anytime model of working – the hybrid model.'	Physical space Temporal space	Multiple locations, time frequency (anytime)

SOURCE	DEFINITION: hybrid work, a hybrid worker	ELEMENTS	SUB-ELEMENTS, FEATURES
MIT Sloan Management Review (e.g., Kane et al., 2021)	'The anticipated gradual return to colocated work in the coming months provides opportunities to experiment with hybrid ways of working … gives managers the ability to critically consider the ways in which a hybrid workplace might be more effective.'	Physical space	Main workplace, effectiveness
International organisations' reports			
ILO, 2021c	'Pre-pandemic research (Eurofound and ILO, 2017) suggests that the "sweet spot" for teleworking is some combination of work at the employer's premises and teleworking. During the pandemic, this approach has come to be known as the "hybrid model"— working part-time in the office combined with part-time telework.'	Physical space Temporal space	Main workplace, multiple locations, duration
OECD, 2021	'In particular, proximity to employers' premises still plays a role for workers in hybrid models, which combine teleworking and office presence, whereas this factor becomes negligible in work-from-anywhere models, which primarily rely on online communication, with personnel distributed across locations and, often, time zones.'	Physical space Virtual space Temporal space	Main workplace, multiple locations, online, timing

Source: Vartiainen and Vanharanta (2023, pp. 26–27).

The comparison of hybrid work definitions in consulting company publications, professional journals and international organisation reports shows that the physical space element – working remotely and in the office – and the temporal element were the most frequent elements used to characterise hybrid work. However, other features, such as flexibility, autonomy, agility, and the choices that autonomy offer an employee, were also included.

HYBRID WORK CONCEPTS IN EUROPE

The hybrid work was much discussed in Europe during the pandemic. In the survey study of the country correspondents (N = 27), they were asked to find:

> Existing definitions of hybrid work or similar concept(s) referring to the situation in which work is performed partly from the employer's premises and partly from other locations, indicating the original designation(s), its source(s), and the main

differences among different concepts, if applicable. (Vartiainen and Vanharanta, 2023, p. 27)

Data and analysis

Altogether, 93 definitions of hybrid work and 14 definitions concerning similar concepts were identified in the country reports. The content of these definitions was analysed using Atlas.ti software. The analysis proceeded in three phases. First, the sources mentioning hybrid work or a similar concept, and who mentioned them, were identified. Not all reports explicitly mentioned 'hybrid work'; traditional remote work and telework definitions were often used. These reports were not included in the analysis. The following actors were identified as the sources of definitions: private sector companies, research institutes, government, public/media, employers, social partners (employers and unions together), unions, consultants and political parties. Second, the core content of each hybrid work definition and definitions related to similar concepts was coded based on the preliminary hybrid work model, as shown in Figure 3.8. The basic elements and their sub-element could include adjustable features such as working at home, using online technologies, communicating face-to-face, and working fixed days at the office each week. For example, some definitions used workplaces as the defining characteristic of hybrid work: 'working in [the] office and [at] home', 'not [a] dedicated workplace in [the] office', and 'working elsewhere'; others referred to time: 'two home days', 'three office days', and 'occasional telework'. New features were also inductively added to the analyses. One definition could include one or more features. The tables in the next section show the elements and sub-elements of hybrid work and their features in the collected definitions, and those of similar concepts. Third, the features defining hybrid work were also grouped into four categories based on flexibility concepts: flexibility in time, work organisation and location, and the emphasis on technology.

Hybrid Work Definitions in the European Discussion

Hybrid work definitions

Physical space and time were the most common basic elements used to define hybrid work (Table 4.2). Social space, virtual space and their sub-elements were sometimes used. However, the definitions included many additional features. Physical space was described in terms of working in multiple locations, especially at the main workplace and home. The quality of workplaces in different locations was almost not discussed. Time was another defining element in answer to the questions of when, for how long, and how often work took place. This meant working at fixed times during the week, month or year at

Table 4.2 *Examples of typical hybrid work definitions (N = 93) and the number of elements, sub-elements, and features mentioned in the excerpts from the correspondents' reports*

EXAMPLE QUOTES	SUB-ELEMENTS	FEATURES
(N = 93)	**PHYSICAL SPACE (N = 79)**	
'Employers' organisation AWVN uses the following definition in a news publication on their website: Hybrid work: "partly at home and partly in the office or elsewhere".'	72 x location 3 x workplace 3 x mobility	48 x multiple locations 28 x main workplace 23 x home 1 x shared office
	TEMPORAL SPACE (N = 43)	
'It has already introduced its "60/40" hybrid working model in Ireland. This allows employees to work 60% of their time remotely and 40% in the office which will allow employees to maintain the flexibility they had during the pandemic.'	22 x timing 13 x duration 9 x time frequency	18 x fixed time, 5 x part-time 4 x days/week 3 x mixed time, occasionally 2 x regularly, weekly 1 x always, hours/day, anytime
	SOCIAL SPACE (N = 11)	
'The Fraunhofer Institute also calls for the hybrid model as an attractive and socially acceptable work arrangement, on the one hand to better ensure the exchange of information and social cohesion in teams/departments, and on the other hand to ensure leadership tasks.'	11 x communication 2 x group maintenance 2 x task-orientation 1 x social relations	10 x face-to-face 2 x mediated communication 1 x alienation, social isolation, trust, leadership
	VIRTUAL SPACE (N = 10)	
'Hybrid work is result-oriented work and leadership based on trust and dialogue. You collaborate with others from different work locations and stay connected through technology and physical meetings.'	10 x virtual space 1 x online	1 x ICT, online tools
	ADDITIONAL FEATURES (N = 38)	
'The office space and how it can be organised in a way that it supports both face-to-face interaction and privacy for online meetings and video calls; the technical equipment necessary to make a hybrid work organisation possible; the organisational culture or working culture are also topics covered in the debate on hybrid work; an ecological perspective, as less work at the office might mean less commuting; debated is also an "alienation" and a loss of creativity.'		11 x autonomy 6 x flexibility 5 x agreement 3 x job content, performance 2 x based on needs, based on company decisions, contract 1 x creativity, ecology, organisation culture, well-being

Source: Vartiainen and Vanharanta (2023, p. 29).

the office and remotely; for example, three office days and two telework days each week. Social space was discussed regarding how communication and collaborative interaction were arranged. Usually, the meaning and significance of face-to-face contact were underlined, and sometimes related to building trust and leadership and avoiding social isolation and alienation. Virtual space was also sometimes – though not in all cases – referred to as the basic element of hybrid work. Autonomy, flexibility, agreements and contracts were considered additional features of hybrid work. It was also expected that in organising hybrid work, features of job content and performance, employees' needs and organisational culture, well-being, and ecological issues, should be considered.

Similar concepts

Smart working, agile work, flexible work, blended working, and similar concepts were defined with the same basic elements as hybrid work, and mostly in terms of the physical space, time and virtual space elements, as shown in Table 4.3. The physical space of work in the future was characterised as working in multiple locations, at home, and at the main workplace. In terms of time, this was characterised by decisions about when work would take place (timing) and for how long (duration). Virtual space was only referred to in terms of data safety. In addition, future work was defined as having different forms and being autonomous, flexible and non-hierarchical. In some definitions, it was also described as being based on the organisation's goals, values and written agreements, and as crossing the organisation's constraints and boundaries.

For example, one respondent defined 'workation', referring to working in distant locations, as follows:

> A working model in which the employer arranges for employees to work abroad or in a resort city in the same country, where part of the time is devoted to doing work, part of the time is devoted to professional self-development, and part of the time is for rest. (Example quote)

Flexibility Perspective on Hybrid Work

The hybrid work definitions were also categorised by flexibility in time, flexibility in work organisation, flexibility in using different locations, and technology options-related issues. Information and communication technology (ICT) use was seldom mentioned as a feature of hybrid work. Most interesting were the definitions that added new features to time and physical space elements and organisation. Actors such as representatives of private sector companies, governments and research institutes were the main sources of definitions. In addition, representatives of trade unions and news in public media provided definitions.

Table 4.3 *Examples of similar concepts and the number of elements, sub-elements, and features in the correspondents' reports*

<table>
<tr><th>SIMILAR CONCEPTS (N = 14)</th><th>EXAMPLE QUOTES</th><th>SUB-ELEMENTS</th><th>FEATURES</th></tr>
<tr><td rowspan="9">• Full-time telework organisation
• Agile work
• 'Crossbreed' work
• Smart working
• A form of telework
• A mixed work model
• Partial teleworking
• Workation
• Flexible organisation
• Boundless work
• Working from home
• Blended working
• Flexible ways of working
• Regular telework</td><td rowspan="9">'Hence, what in the international debate and legislation is expressed more generically with the term Remote Work or Hybrid Work, implying a work carried out outside the office, whether stably, at regular or occasional intervals, in Italy is referred to as Smart Working or Agile Work.'
'The Tánaiste and Minister for Enterprise, Trade and Employment, Leo Varadkar, said that blended working will involve working sometimes from the office and other times from home, a hub or on the go.'
'There are no other official definitions of hybrid work nor other similar definitions. In parallel to hybrid work, a term "flexible work" (a flexible way of working) (in Swedish "flexibelt arbetssätt") is sometimes used to describe not only to non-place-based work but also the wider flexibilization of work (e.g., in terms of working hours).'</td><td colspan="2">PHYSICAL SPACE (N = 15)</td></tr>
<tr><td>12 x location
5 x workplace</td><td>12 x multiple locations
2 x home
2 x work as environment
1 x main workplace</td></tr>
<tr><td colspan="2">TEMPORAL SPACE (N = 11)</td></tr>
<tr><td>4 x timing
2 x duration
2 x time frequency</td><td></td></tr>
<tr><td colspan="2">SOCIAL SPACE (N = 1)</td></tr>
<tr><td></td><td>1 x organisation constraints and contexts</td></tr>
<tr><td colspan="2">VIRTUAL SPACE (N = 1)</td></tr>
<tr><td></td><td>1 x data safety</td></tr>
<tr><td colspan="2">ADDITIONAL FEATURES (N = 15)
5 x flexibility
3 x autonomy
1 x written agreement, organisational objectives, variety of forms, non-hierarchical, work–life balance, organisational constraints and boundaries, value-based drivers</td></tr>
</table>

Source: Vartiainen and Vanharanta (2023, pp. 30–31).

Flexibility in time

Flexibility related to time was referred to most often. *Temporal flexibility* indicators varied from generic occasional and part-time telework, and a fixed number of days per week at the office, to adjustable timeshares between the office, home and elsewhere, for example: two days at home and three days at the office; 50 per cent in-office work and 50 per cent at-home work scheduled between 7 am and 8 pm; rotating amounts of office work between 30 per cent and 70 per cent; a maximum of 35 days of working from home per year; or alternating between one week at the office and one week elsewhere.

> Under the new model, 50 per cent of working time must be spent in the office, but employees can schedule their working time between 7 am and 8 pm as they please when working from home. (Example quote)

Flexibility in work organisation

Flexibility in organising refers to ways of flexibly organising features of hybrid work. The definitions included several elements and features, such as who has the decision-making power – for example, the employee, the manager or the company – the location of the work, and the work schedule. In addition, other options influencing the manifestation of hybridity were mentioned, such as flexible choices and agreements based on job responsibilities, the need for communication and interaction, and company and job needs:

> Hybrid work relies on the possibility of choosing flexibly the location from which the work is done. It is not the building or office that is decisive, but the type of work to be done, the necessary communication possibilities and the degree of interaction. In a hybrid work environment, work at the office is combined with work from home, or any other location. (Example quotation)

Flexibility in location

In many quotations, the flexible choice of location was the main element of hybrid work, referring quite often to only the employer's premises and some other places. *Location flexibility* indicators varied from generic, such as 'working elsewhere' or at on-site and off-site locations, to more specific, such as offices and homes and mobile, multilocational and hub work inside one country; teleworking abroad for a certain period was also mentioned.

> Hybrid work is mostly defined as working on the employer's premises and in other locations (Example quote).

Technological options

Technology played only a minor role in these definitions. However, the need to enable presence, awareness of others, and virtual connectivity from anywhere and the need for the employee and employer to agree about who bears responsibility for providing ICT use opportunities were emphasised.

> The hybrid organisation combines physical presence with work from other locations, such as homework. This means that some parts of the company's tasks are performed virtually, while others are performed by meeting physically (Example quote).

It can be concluded that the definitions of hybrid work and similar concepts at the member state level typically mention physical space and time elements and features. Even when the concepts differed, their content was similar. For example, 'blended working' was defined as working sometimes from the office and other times from home, at a hub or on the go. This definition is reminiscent of the concept of multilocational work. The analysis of the definitions in the excerpts from the viewpoint of flexibility confirms this conclusion.

ADDITIONAL FEATURES TO THE HYBRID WORK MODEL

The preliminary hybrid work model gains some new features based on the findings of the literature and country report analyses (Figure 4.1). Based on them, it can be concluded that hybrid work is more than just combining working regularly in the office and elsewhere. It is flexible. The analysis of hybrid work definitions presented in the literature and country reports during the pandemic shows that the physical space element (remote work in multiple locations and working at the main workplace) and the temporal element (that is, when, for how long and how often work is done in each location and workplace), were the elements most frequently used to characterise hybrid work. In these definitions, social and virtual elements were used only occasionally. The same pattern of elements was found for definitions of close concepts. When the hybrid work definitions in the recent literature and country reports are compared with the earlier definitions of remote work and telework, we can see that they use the same basic elements, although the former are more streamlined.

In the European Framework Agreement (ETUC et al., 2002), telework is defined as:

> A form of organising and/or performing work, using information technology, in the context of an employment contract/relationship, where work, which could also be performed at the employer's premises, is carried out away from those premises on a regular basis.

This definition of telework includes physical space (location), virtual space (ICT) and time (time frequency) elements in addition to referring to a feature of an employment contract or relationship.

Later, telework and ICT-based mobile work were defined (Eurofound, 2020, p. 1) as:

> Telework and ICT-based mobile work (TICTM) is any type of work arrangement where workers work remotely, away from an employer's premises or fixed location, using digital technologies such as networks, laptops, mobile phones and the internet.

The International Labour Organization (ILO, 2020c, p. 6) defined telework as:

> A subcategory of the broader concept of remote work. It includes workers who use information and communications technology (ICT) or landline telephones to carry out the work remotely. Similar to remote work, telework can be carried out in different locations outside the default place of work. What makes telework a unique category is that the work carried out remotely includes the use of personal electronic devices.

These definitions of remote work and telework, and ICT-based mobile work, include only physical space (excluding the main workplace) and virtual space (ICT) elements in addition to the feature of flexible arrangements.

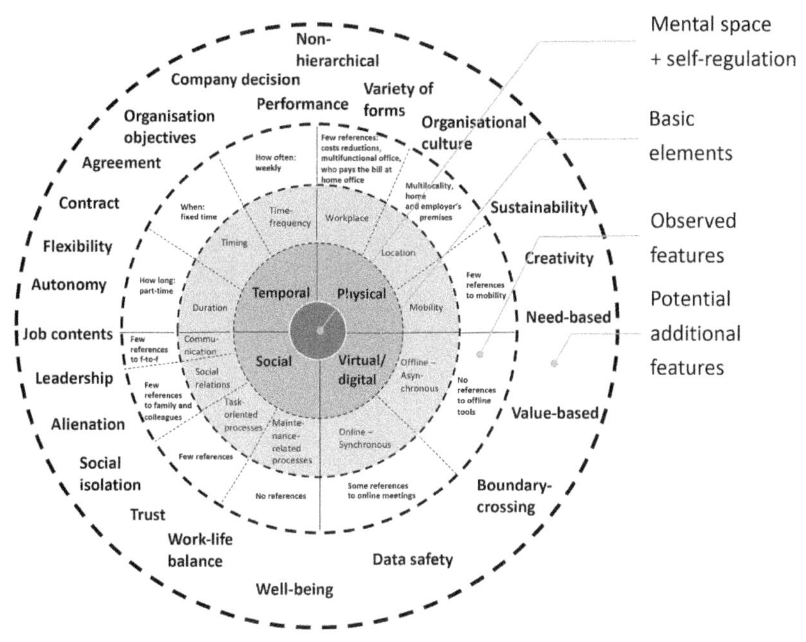

Source: Vartiainen and Vanharanta (2023, p. 34).

Figure 4.1 *An extended hybrid work model: potential addition features named in the literature and country reports to the preliminary hybrid work model's basic and sub-elements (outer circle). The observed features are shown in the inner circle*

Figure 4.1 shows that virtual and social elements are almost entirely missing from the definitions of hybrid work produced during the pandemic. This is evocative of the 'classical' definitions of remote work, telework and ICT-based mobile work, although the newer definitions include virtuality. However, as for the physical spaces, the discussion on workplaces called attention to the costs of premises both at the office and home; 'location' sometimes implied multi-locality, but was only seldom linked to mobility. In the virtual space, there were surprisingly few references to digital tools. Few references to social space focused on the importance of face-to-face meetings and social support from colleagues and family. As for the time element, this mostly referred to fixed-term, weekly working on certain days.

The main differences between the definitions of hybrid work and similar concepts, and earlier definitions of remote work and telework, are evident in the additional features they propose and use. First, the newer definitions underline flexibility and autonomy in arrangements of physical and temporal spaces. Second, they characterise hybrid work with more detailed – but individualised – features. These individualised features highlight the need for developing contracts and agreements; preventing isolation and alienation; providing support for well-being, work–life balance and creativity; and investing in developing leadership. This indicates that changing job responsibilities and working environments impact upon how hybrid work is designed and implemented in organisations and practised locally and flexibly. Finally, the additional features also reflect the potential and opportunities of future flexible hybrid work.

NOTE

1. The study 'Hybrid work – challenges, opportunities and risks post-pandemic' was funded by the European Foundation for the Improvement of Living and Working Conditions (Eurofound), project 190302.

5. Potential hindrances and challenges

When designing, implementing and further developing hybrid work, it is vital to identify the possible hindrances and challenges of the work that can slow down the hybrid change and negatively affect or limit the employees' well-being and commitment as well as the organisation's performance. This chapter focuses, first, on identifying hindrances and challenges in traditional remote work and telework literature, and then on the expectations related to hybrid work during the pandemic. Their identification opens the road to transform them into benefits and developmental opportunities for actors when additional job-related, social and personal resources are granted (Chapter 6).

While the perceived hindrances and challenges during the pandemic were related to the extreme case of obligatory telework from home, they provide important insights into telework management and what needs to be considered when planning and implementing the hybrid model. In addition, pre-pandemic research on remote work and telework is central to building an understanding of the requirements of home working (HW) organisation. Therefore, this chapter focuses on the following question: What are the expected hindrances and challenges related to hybrid work, and what should be focused on when designing and implementing hybrid work?

HINDRANCES AND CHALLENGES AS JOB DEMANDS

Potential hindrances and challenges (and in Chapter 6, also benefits and opportunities) in hybrid work are reviewed by using *the job demands–resources (JD-R) model* (Bakker, 2011; Demerouti et al., 2001; Bakker and Demerouti, 2017) as the framework. In the JD-R model, job demands represent characteristics that potentially evoke strain and influence performance if they exceed the employee's adaptive resources (Bakker et al., 2007), that is, job and personal resources. This is possible in hybrid work when the physical, virtual, social and temporal aspects of a job change during the transition, and require adjustment to a new context and a new psychological orientation and the ways of coping. Job demands in hybrid work are objective, determinable elements and features of work and in the working environment. For example, location flexibility allows high mobility and use of different locations if needed, and time flexibility allows scheduling work autonomously within certain time limits. For designing and implementing hybrid work, it is important to notice the expected hindrances and challenges, as work demands can be influenced, compensated for and strategically navigated.

Job demands in the JD-R model are often divided into two categories: hindrance-related and challenge-related demands (e.g., Cavanaugh et al., 2000; Van den Broeck et al., 2010). *Challenge demands* are work characteristics that stimulate individuals to put effort into the task and help to achieve goals. They create opportunities for personal growth, learning and achievement. However, changing work demands can also include interruptions, disturbances and other hurdles resulting from the new context that can hinder work actions. According to recent studies, job demands that employees perceive as hindrances are positively associated with exhaustion, and negatively associated with vigour (Van den Broeck et al., 2010) and work engagement (Crawford et al., 2010). *Hindering job demands* in work circumstances involves excessive or undesirable constraints that interfere with or inhibit an actor's ability to achieve important goals. For example, changing work contexts in mobile work often include interruptions in shared workspaces, disturbances in communication with colleagues and management, and other hurdles that hinder individual work actions. However, research has also shown that challenges may be experienced as hindrance demands (and vice versa) depending on the context (Bakker and Demerouti, 2017). Therefore, it is important to notice that challenge demands are not inherently a negative aspect of hybrid work. However, they may result in hindrances if the resources an employee has at their disposal are not sufficient to support the worker in meeting the challenges (Bakker and Demerouti, 2017). Hindrances can also be overcome.

JOB DEMANDS IN REMOTE WORK AND TELEWORK BEFORE AND DURING THE PANDEMIC

Hindrances and Challenges of Traditional Remote and Telework

Bailey and Kurland (2002) refer to the review of Pinsonneault and Boisvert (2001) examining the literature on the negative and positive impacts of teleworking from the 1990s and earlier. It informed about the following *negative impacts of telecommuting* on individuals: feelings of professional and social isolation, reduction in chances of promotion, tendencies to overwork, and potential decrease in the frequency of intra-organisational communication for full-time telecommuters. The topics are similar to the present-day discussion on hybrid work, although they were observed almost three decades ago. Boell et al.'s (2013) literature review adds to this list of challenges: blurring work–life, reducing trust, reduced technical support, increased technical problems, and unwanted interruptions. However, in empirical studies, the impacts have been found to be controversial and ambiguous, since remote work does not directly affect outcomes, but does so through several modifying factors. For example, in their meta-analysis, Gajendran and Harrison (2007) did not find negative consequences except that high-intensity telecommuting (more than 2.5 days a week) accentuated telecommuting's beneficial effects on work–family conflict, but harmed relationships with co-workers. Some generic impacts, however, are repeatedly presented.

One's home also being one's workplace is implicit in a telework context (Raghuram et al., 2019). A central challenge discussed in the telework literature is thus the management of the *work–family* interface (Beauregard et al., 2019; Biron and Van Veldhoven, 2016; Boell et al., 2013; Tremblay and Thomsin, 2012) – or more generally speaking, the work–life balance – and the potential hindrances resulting from the blurring of the spatial and temporal boundaries of these two areas of life. Allen et al. (2015) found a small positive association between telecommuting and work–family conflict. Work-related hindrances associated with the blurring of work and family life include stress and concentration issues due to distractions from the home environment (Galanti et al., 2021). In addition, Camacho and Barrios (2022) found that two technostressors (work–home conflict and work overload) generated strain in teleworkers, decreasing their satisfaction with telework and perceived job performance. 'Technostress' refers to a situation of stress that an individual experiences due to their use of information technology (IT) (Tarafdar et al., 2019). Technostress resulting, for example, from constant floods of notifications, can negatively influence well-being and impair cognitive abilities (Salo et al., 2022).

Teleworkers experience the challenge of *social isolation* because of decreased in-person interaction with colleagues and superiors, and increased reliance on technology-mediated communication (Beauregard et al., 2019; Biron and Van Veldhoven, 2016; Boell et al., 2013; Charalampous et al., 2019; Gajendran and Harrison, 2007; Raghuram et al., 2019; Tremblay and Thomsin, 2012). Such social and professional isolation in an organisation has been identified as hindering informal learning and feedback, and resulting in perceived career stagnation, emotional exhaustion, cognitive stress and weakening of social relationships (Beauregard et al., 2019; Biron and Van Veldhoven, 2016; Charalampous et al., 2019).

In addition, *trust* issues reflected by increased monitoring by management have been reported (Boell et al., 2013; Charalampous et al., 2019). This led to a proposal (Suder and Siibak, 2022) to draft national laws to strengthen the possibility for employees to opt out of such applications and technologies, after the end of the COVID-19 pandemic.

Additionally, issues related to *physical well-being*, such as musculoskeletal problems due to poor ergonomics (Charalampous et al., 2019), are identified by researchers as potential hindrances in telework. Working outside the company premises has also been associated with increased interruptions and technical problems hindering work (Boell et al., 2013).

On the *organisational level*, Pinsonneault and Boisvert (2001) identified in their literature review the following *negative impacts*: greater absence of the best employees from the office; loss of synergy in the organisation; difficulty in managing telecommuting, making supervisors dissatisfied; increased data security concerns; and difficulty in objectively evaluating the financial benefits of telecommuting. The financial organisational benefits are related to performance outcomes of remote and telework. De Menezes and Kelliher (2011), in their review of 148 studies on flexible working arrangements (FWAs) and performance, largely failed to demonstrate the relationship between FWAs and outcomes in general. Later, Boell et al. (2013) raised some additional issues in organisations considering remote and telework: management practices must shift away from direct supervision to management by objectives, and the legal framework of telework may be missing and should be developed. In addition, teamwork and collaboration may be more difficult, and organisations and their staff may miss some expertise; infrastructure and technologies are not sufficient; and data security is limited. The transformation to remote and telework also requires monetary investment in technology and people. At the organisational level, central challenges include the monitoring of employees (Beauregard et al., 2019), thereby raising the need for management approaches focusing on outcomes rather than presence (Aloisi and De Stefano, 2022). In addition, means of ensuring knowledge transfer (Beauregard et al., 2019) are needed, and the development of organisational teamwork and the facilitation of interactions among employees. The challenges must be met related to the maintenance of information and communication technology (ICT) infrastructure and data security (Boell et al., 2013).

Hindrances and Challenges During the Pandemic

During the pandemic, remote and telework was mainly done from home, which raised questions about the usability of the home as a workplace, and the family as a social work environment; about the functionality of means of communication to promote social relations with colleagues and superiors; and about the availability and usefulness of technologies in work and collaboration. A survey (Ipsen et al., 2021) from 29 European countries on knowledge workers' (N = 5748) experiences of working from home confirmed that the main concerns were home office constraints, work uncertainties and inadequate tools. These findings were gender-related, as the male respondents could work more effectively and efficiently from home; they felt less constrained by their home office, and missed necessary work tools less than the women. The employees with children at home felt the home office constraints more than the people without children.

Experiences related to *social isolation, including loneliness*, increased compared to the time before the pandemic, and the quality of social relationships deteriorated (Buecker and Horstmann, 2021). Many studies revealed that many housework and intensive childcare demands were imposed on families and remote workers. Parents and caretakers' access to help for domestic and care work, paid or unpaid, was limited because of mandatory stay-at-home orders and social distancing (Parlak et al., 2021; Risi and Pronzato, 2021). Intensified housework and childcare negatively influenced remote workers' ability to concentrate on work-related tasks, and imposed additional demands on working parents, leading to experiences of work–family imbalance. For example, Shirmohammadi et al. (2022), in their synthesis of factors influencing work–life balance, observed that although flexibility in the timing and execution of tasks enhanced employees' perceived autonomy, telework during the pandemic was accompanied by work intensification and increased working hours. Remote and telework also implicitly involve locational flexibility; however, space limitations have become challenging for many remote workers. In addition, although working from home allows for flexible roles and scheduling of family matters, in practice, families and remote workers were faced with a huge amount of housework and intense childcare demands.

A study in Asia (Gibbs et al., 2021) used data from over 10 000 IT professionals both before and during the working-from-home period during the pandemic. Working outside normal business hours rose 18 per cent from levels before the pandemic, and average output declined slightly; thus, productivity fell 8–19 per cent. Employees with children at home increased their work hours more and had a larger decline in productivity than those without children. Women had a larger decline in productivity, while those with longer company tenure fared better. One source of these changes in productivity was higher communication and coordination costs; time spent on coordination activities and meetings increased, while uninterrupted work hours shrank considerably.

The adoption rates of videoconferencing increased significantly in 2020, predominantly because videoconferencing somewhat resembles face-to-face interaction, and using it decreased commuting. One of the most serious critiques concerned the limits to generating creative ideas while having videoconference meetings. Brucks and Levav (2022) showed that videoconferencing can inhibit the production of creative ideas. However, when selecting which idea to pursue, they found no evidence that videoconferencing groups are less effective (and preliminary evidence that they may be more effective) than in-person groups. Ideation is therefore more difficult, but after finding an idea, working on it further is not. They explained the decreased idea generation by a narrower cognitive focus on interaction on the screen, instead of a focus on producing ideas.

Hacker et al. (2020) studied the use of web-conferencing systems such as Zoom, applying text mining techniques to Twitter data collecting 3 million tweets. They identified five affordances and constraints to the use of collaboration systems. In all, they found that videoconferencing enabled people to have encounters that could not be possible otherwise because of the pandemic. Affordances were related to communicating with social groups – for example, colleagues – and engaging in shared social activities with them. In addition, it was possible to attend virtual events, for example, a concert; to pursue hobbies, for example, online yoga classes; and to consume non-recreational services, for example, to get career advice. Along with the benefits, some challenges were observed. Videoconferencing was also found to have well-being outcomes. Teleworkers complained about the shortcomings in technological features – for example, how to record a meeting – and skills to use technologies. People also found it challenging to comply with norms and habits; for example, how to dress for virtual meetings. To be always 'on' resulted in *'Zoom fatigue'*. Working from home also generated feelings about exposing one's private living space to view. Privacy and security issues were also brought up.

The hindrances and challenges were related to communication, collaboration, and using technologies to replace face-to-face meetings. Though information and communication technologies make remote work possible, the pandemic highlighted *technostress* and isolation as two major challenges that employees working from home confronted while depending on ICTs in order to work. For example, Yang et al. (2022) studied the effects of firm-wide remote work on collaboration and communication at US Microsoft (N = 61 182) over the first six months of the pandemic. They found that the collaboration networks of workers became more static and siloed, with fewer bridges between disparate parts; synchronous communication decreased, and asynchronous communication increased. Many of these challenges can be explained by the affordance limits of technologies. For example, Fauville et al. (2021) found while developing and validating the Zoom Exhaustion and Fatigue Scale that the higher the frequency, duration and 'burstiness' of Zoom meetings were, the higher the level of fatigue experienced; and fatigue was associated with negative attitudes towards Zoom meetings. This phenomenon is called 'Zoom fatigue' or more generally *'videoconference fatigue'*.

Riedl (2022, p. 157) defined the concept of Zoom fatigue or videoconference fatigue as: 'somatic and cognitive exhaustion that is caused by the intensive and/or inappropriate use of videoconferencing tools, frequently accompanied by related symptoms such as tiredness, worry, anxiety, burnout, discomfort, and stress, as well as other bodily symptoms such as headaches'. He also presented six root reasons for fatigue (Figure 5.1). The decrease in a communication medium's naturalness, that is, lack of information and information overload, lead to increased cognitive effort and hence to videoconferencing fatigue. What, then, can be done? For the design collaboration technologies, Bergmann et al. (2023) argue that videoconferencing design should move away from designing for steady states, and towards designing to embrace change, and helping teams to motivate accountable choices about working together in ways that embrace both effectiveness and sociality. For using technologies, Riedl (2022, p. 166) suggests 17 practices grouped into three categories: organisational countermeasures (etiquette), personal behavioural rules to avoid stress, and use of software features designed to imitate better face-to-face interaction.

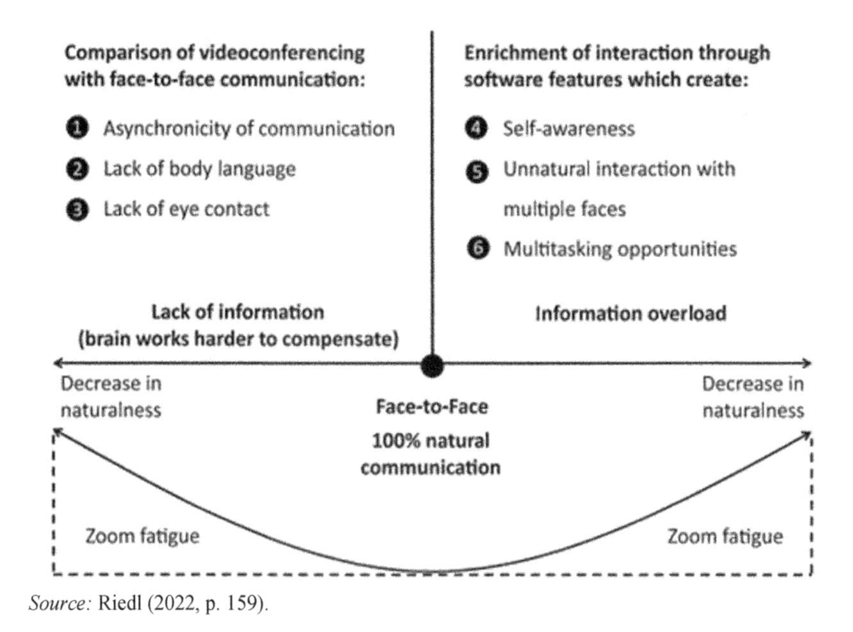

Source: Riedl (2022, p. 159).

Figure 5.1 Six root causes and decreases in the naturalness of videoconferencing and Zoom fatigue

EXPECTED HINDRANCES AND CHALLENGES OF HYBRID WORK IN EUROPE

In addition to studying the immediate impacts of the transition to obligatory telework from home, the expectations regarding the potential hindrances and challenges of future hybrid work were explored by using the European survey data collected from 27 European countries (Vartiainen and Vanharanta, 2023). The study was done by analysing the contents of country reports and linked reports concerning the expectations of the various actors, including social partners, managers, and the media. *As expected, there were many similarities with the earlier studies*. Next, the expectations of different actors regarding the impacts of HW on the individual, team, organisation, and society levels are shown and discussed. The analysis concerned the question: What hindrances and challenges were expected from hybrid work after the pandemic?

Analysis

Hindrances and challenges were analysed as the expected impacts of future hybrid work. First, the type and content of impacts were identified, after which the level of impact – that is, employee (workers, superiors), organisation (management) and society – were coded using the definitions listed below:

- *Hindrances:* the kinds of hindrances that implementing HW arrangements could present for individuals, teams, organisations, and so on.
- *Challenges:* the kinds of challenges that implementing HW arrangements could present for individuals, teams, organisations, and so on.
- *Level of impact:* who is impacted by the implementation of HW; that is, individuals (employees, superiors), teams, organisations (management) and society.

Findings

On the employee level, hindrances were related to social relations, well-being and work–life balance. Individual-level challenges were related to HW agreements and social relations at work. Only a few hindrances and challenges could be observed on the team level. On the organisation level, a few hindrances were mentioned, but tensions related to challenges and opportunities to develop agreements, ICT, physical premises, and leadership were mostly identified. On the societal level, labour relations, health and well-being, and cost issues were identified as challenges. The categories and frequency of the expected hindrances and challenges of hybrid work for individuals, teams, organisations and society are summarised in Table 5.1.

Hindrances

Most of the expected hindrances (N = 38) are at the *individual level*. The majority are related to a lack of social interaction (for example, feelings of isolation), negative effects on health and well-being (for example, mental health problems), work–life balance issues (for example, difficulties in managing

Table 5.1 The topics and number of expected hindrances and challenges in hybrid work on the individual, team, organisation, and society levels

HINDRANCES (N = 38)	CHALLENGES (N = 99)
Employees (workers, superiors)	
Social relations (N = 4), health and well-being (N = 4), work–life balance (N = 3), inequality (N = 3), workload (N = 2), costs (N = 2), ICT (N = 2), other: loss of creativity, motivation, data security, precarity, availability of knowledge, surveillance, alienation, taxes	HW agreements (N = 11), social relations (N = 8), employment relations (N = 5), leadership (N = 5), work–life balance (N = 4), workload (N = 4), working conditions (N = 3), career (N = 2), ICT (N = 2), inequality (N = 2), other: mindset, communication, competence, health and well-being, legislation, location, office, productivity, recruitment, trade union membership, work culture
Team	
Alienation	HW agreements (N = 2), communication (N = 2), workload (N = 2)
Organisation (management viewpoint)	
Social relations, motivation, work–life balance, health and well-being, surveillance	Leadership (N = 4), HW agreements (N = 4), social relations (N = 4), working conditions (N = 2), employment relationship (N = 2), other: communication, costs, health and well-being, ICT, inequality, office, privacy
Society	
Inequality, costs, taxes, knowledge	Employment relationship (N = 3), health and well-being (N = 2), costs (N = 2), other: social relations, working conditions, mindset, communication, implementation, knowledge, office, productivity

Source: Vartiainen and Vanharanta (2023, pp. 49–50).

the boundaries of these two domains), and inequality (for example, women's dual role in domestic work and occupation). In addition, increased workload, and costs such as the inability to purchase work desks and ICT at home, were identified as hindrances associated with hybrid work. On the *team and organisation levels*, some remarks about the lack of social relations, reduced motivation, problems maintaining work–life balance, and negative effects on health and well-being, as well as surveillance exercised by the employer through technologies, were made. On the *societal level*, inequality, knowledge about employees' rights and responsibilities, and the costs and taxes associated with teleworking from home, were highlighted. The survey data from Romania in February 2021 reveals that four out of ten women said that their work–life balance had deteriorated; in some cases, they had had to work harder, including overtime, to meet the requirements, but also because some housework took up more time than usual. In a Dutch financial daily newspaper, a professor of leadership and organisational change found that hybrid working increased women's housework, and that women in Dutch academia began publishing fewer articles than usual during forced telework periods.

Challenges

Challenges (N = 99) expected in hybrid work also appeared mostly at the *individual level*, and included issues related to: agreeing on the conditions of hybrid work, for example, work expenses outside the office to create proper working conditions, including ICT; employment relationships, including the rights and responsibilities of teleworking employees; and career prospects (Table 5.1). The expected challenges in social relations concentrated on maintaining relations with co-workers. In addition, the quality of leadership, increased workload, and balancing work and other areas of life were expected to be challenges in hybrid work. On the *team level*, maintaining a sense of community, ensuring appropriate workload, and lacking agreement between employees and employers concerning, for example, working time, appeared as challenges. On the *organisational level*, challenges were mostly related to the quality of the management and leadership of remote workers, work contracts defining the employment relationship, and proper working conditions, including social ties with co-workers. Similar challenges to be overcome – that is, how employment relations, working conditions and expenses should be arranged and how to guarantee the well-being of remote workers and teleworkers – were found at the *societal level.*

EXPECTED FEATURES OF HYBRID WORK

The hindrances and challenges of remote work and telework identified earlier and during the pandemic literature, and those brought up in country reports, have – as expected – several similarities. They differ in which hindrances and challenges are accentuated, and what perspectives consider them most relevant. However, they are also controversial, as empirical studies sometimes confirm the impacts and sometimes do not. This can be explained by versatile applications of remote and telework in practice. Job contents and demands dynamically vary in physical, social, virtual and temporal spaces, as well as available resources; many moderating factors influence the outcomes (e.g., de Menezes and Kelliher, 2011).

Ambivalent and Contradictory Implications for Hybrid Work

One significant factor influencing the outcomes is the intensity of telework; that is, working full-time or part-time. Many hindrances and challenges identified in earlier telework literature are associated with high-intensity telework, the primary working mode. At the same time, low intensity refers to a maximum of 2.5 days of telework per week (Gajendran and Harrison, 2007). Some benefits have a curvilinear relationship with telework intensity; whereas some challenges and benefits are accentuated as the intensity of telework increases. For example, Biron and Van Veldhoven (2016) demonstrate that in high-intensity teleworking, isolation negatively influences performance, but in part-time teleworking, the influence of isolation on performance is negligible. Similarly, the review by Beauregard et al. (2019) indicates that high-intensity teleworking is associated with negative implications for career advancement. In contrast, low-intensity telework has not influenced social relations and career advancement. Studies also show some positive implications of telework levelling off as the intensity of telework increases. For example, Biron and Van Veldhoven (2016) show how increases in job satisfaction drop off as teleworking becomes more extensive. The same phenomenon has been found in relation to autonomy. Gajendran and Harrison's (2007) meta-analysis shows how both high- and low-intensity telecommuters experience similar levels of autonomy, which suggests that after an initial increase in the perception of autonomy accruing from 1–2 days of telework, there is only a marginal increase in feelings of autonomy as time spent telecommuting increases.

Telework reviews also point out several inconsistent arguments and ambivalences related to the implications of telework, illustrating how the same aspect of telework may be considered a demand or an advantage. For example, as pointed out above, physical distance from colleagues may result in social and professional isolation and thus have negative implications on relationships and well-being (Bentley et al., 2021). While the opportunity to work in a distraction-free environment is considered to increase concentration, and thereby productivity, the implications on productivity of the lack of interaction and knowledge sharing with colleagues may be harmful (e.g., Beauregard et al., 2019). In addition, using one's home as one's workplace may also lead to distractions (Boell et al., 2013). To maintain contact and meet job expectations, teleworkers rely on ICT, which enables them to stay connected with their work community when working from different locations. This, however, may result in technostress (Beauregard et al., 2019) and exhaustion, longer working hours and difficulties in switching off from work, thus intensifying a culture where individuals are expected to be constantly available (e.g., Derks et al., 2015). Technostress is the mental outcome of the increased use of ICTs. It occurs when a teleworker cannot cope with the situation because using technologies can lead to application multitasking, constant connectivity, information overload and technical problems (Camacho and Barrios, 2022). In the long run, this can translate into health issues if individuals have difficulty in switching off from work and allocating time for recovery (Biron and Van Veldhoven, 2016). Thus, temporal and spatial autonomy, which are associated with various positive implications for individuals, may result in the intensification of work and thereby hamper well-being, leading to the autonomy paradox (Mazmanian et al., 2013) that stems from working and using technologies everywhere and all the time, thus diminishing autonomy in practice.

The main hindrances and challenges of remote work and telework and related expectations concerning hybrid work are outlined in Figure 5.2.

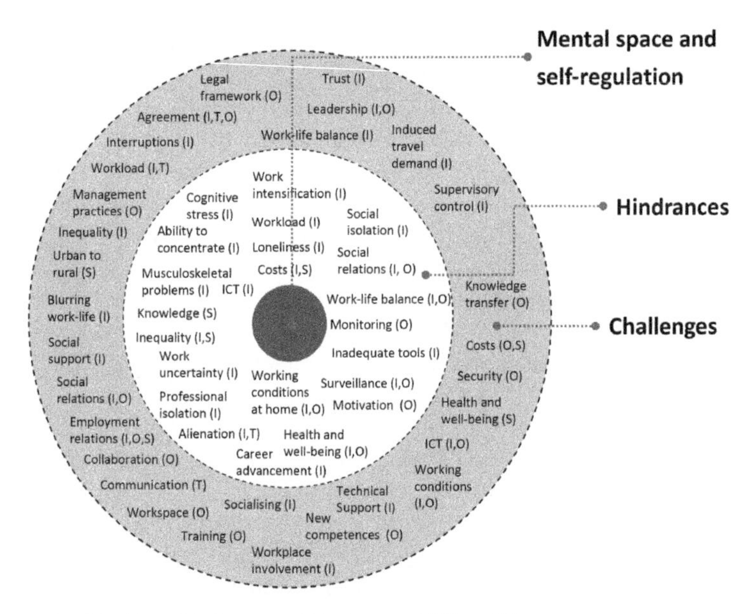

Source: Modified from Vartiainen and Vanharanta (2023, p. 52).

Figure 5.2 Summary of hindrances and challenges on different levels (I = individual, T = team, O = organisation, and S = society) in the remote work and telework literature and country reports regarding expectations on hybrid work

6. Potential benefits and opportunities

EMPLOYEES AND EMPLOYERS ARE LOOKING FOR BENEFITS

Willingness to work in a hybrid manner is common among employees. Surveyed in March 2022, over 60 per cent of respondents in Europe (Eurofound, 2023), both women and men, preferred to work from home at least several times per month; signalling the gap between those who would like to telework and those who do so today. This difference is also shown in a recent global survey (Aksoy et al., 2023) comparing 34 English-speaking, Asian, European and Latin American countries and South Africa on the willingness of employees and employers to work from home. While employees would like to work from home (WFH) on average 2.0 days per week around the globe, employers only plan 1.1 WFH days per week. The gap is largest in Latin America and South Africa, where employees would like to work on average 1.3 days more from home than their employers plan. The gap is smallest in the English-speaking countries, where it amounts to 0.7 days on average. The largest gaps are in Argentina (1.6 days), Brazil (1.2) and Mexico (1.2), while the smallest gaps are in Japan (0.2), the Netherlands (0.3) and Denmark (0.4). Although these figures only apply to working from home and not to other possible locations, this gap speaks to the different attitudes and expectations of employees and employers regarding hybrid work arrangements and their benefits.

In the early stages of telecommuting (Nilles, 1975), reduced travelling, and balancing work and family duties, were expected to be benefits. However, the past years have shown that telework is a multifaceted and complex entity with multiple reasons for implementation, and moderating factors generating controversial impacts. Therefore, this chapter focuses on the following questions: What are the benefits of remote and telework, and what is expected from hybrid work?

Traditional remote and telework literature has identified various individual and organisational benefits related to telework, and explored their relationship with the specific individual- and organisation-level outcomes. To identify the most proximal benefits, existing reviews of telework literature are analysed next. The reviews discuss research evidence on the influence of remote work and telework on topics such as performance, commitment, work–life balance, social relationships, emotions, and physical and mental well-being, as well as on professional isolation and perceptions of career advancement. In addition, some organisational and societal implications have been discussed, although earlier research has primarily focused on individual-level implications (Raghuram et al., 2019). The reviews also include a few recent telework studies conducted during the pandemic to understand the experiences and implications of high-intensity telework, mainly from home. Several studies have sought to explore the implications for motivation, performance and retention, and collaboration, during involuntary telework. In addition, of special interest have been both the level of telework that employees are willing to continue after the COVID-19 pandemic, and organisations' willingness to provide such opportunities.

BENEFITS OF REMOTE WORK AND TELEWORK BEFORE AND DURING THE PANDEMIC

Benefits of Traditional Remote and Telework

Since Nilles (1975), telecommuting – that is, teleworking from home and nearby – has been hailed as a way to lower transportation costs for employees and organisations, reduce environmental pollution and traffic jams, and create a work–life balance by increasing the ability to coordinate work and non-work tasks while teleworking. The same topics also prevail in the later – and present – discussion. Stronger evidence of teleworking's benefits exists where multiple reviews show consistent results. Therefore, they are used below to identify benefits.

Pinsonneault and Boisvert's (2001) review examined the impacts of teleworking from the 1990s and earlier. It informed about the following *positive impacts on individuals*: reduced or even eliminated transport time, cost savings related to work habits (for example, travel, clothing and food), flexibility in the organisation of work hours and leisure activities, and increased productivity, because employees may be able to work in an environment with fewer distractions and use time saved on commuting productively. Increased individual autonomy – that is, teleworkers have more freedom in how they structure their work – has been considered the key advantage from the employee viewpoint. Bailey and Kurland (2002) confirmed that the most important benefits of telework are schedule flexibility, freedom from interruptions, and saving commuting time. Boell et al. (2013), ten years later in their summary of telework literature, added the opportunity for spatial mobility to the list of advantages on the individual level. Participation in work is possible from different locations, such as rural areas. In addition, increased flexibility to manage when, where and how to work can increase job satisfaction. In some other reviews, telework is also associated with improvements in perceived autonomy (Boell et al., 2013; Charalampous et al., 2019; de Menezes and Kelliher, 2011; Gajendran and Harrison, 2007), turnover (Gajendran and Harrison, 2007; McNall et al., 2009), and work interference with family (WIF) (Allen et al., 2013; McNall et al., 2009).

Commuting

Lower transportation costs for employees and organisations, and reduced environmental pollution and traffic jams, have been expected since Nilles (1975). As telework often denotes working from home, it is associated with less commuting and, thereby, the mitigation of stressful demands in the workplace (Biron and Van Veldhoven, 2016). Andreev et al. (2010) reviewed around 100 telecommuting and teleconference studies asking whether using work locations flexibly, and working virtually, eliminate travel. The positive impact is manifested when a location-based activity is substituted by an information and communication (ICT)-based counterpart, thus eliminating travel. They could show that in the short term, telecommuting leads to a reduction in various travel characteristics: for example, vehicle miles travelled, morning peak hours avoided, and number of commuting trips. In the long term, however, the reduction would be much lower due to the induced travel demand: that is, leisure use, and residential relocation. Telework has also been suggested to be beneficial to society by reducing carbon dioxide emissions, and wear and tear on roads, bridges and highway systems, due to reduced commuting (Biron and Van Veldhoven, 2016).

Work–life balance

Kossek and Lautsch (2018) summarised reviews addressing the outcomes of schedule variability that, in principle, enable flexible combinations of work and other life. One review showed that the availability of flexitime practices significantly reduced work interference with family (WIF), but no family interference with work (FIW) was found. However, in another review, both WIF and FIW were reduced, although the effects on the former were stronger.

Stress and well-being

There is a large consensus that telework is associated with significantly lower levels of work-related stress than those experienced by office-based employees. To gain a broad understanding of the association between telework and work-related well-being, Charalampous et al. (2019) focused on reviewed studies of remote knowledge e-workers' well-being at work. They used affective, cognitive, social, occupational and psychosomatic dimensions as indicative affective states of well-being in their analysis. The affective dimension is shown as emotions, job satisfaction, organisational commitment and emotional exhaustion among employees. The cognitive state appears as cognitive weariness, that is, individuals' difficulty in assimilating new information and concentrating. Social well-being refers to the degree to which individuals function well in their social relationships at work. Professional well-being comprises autonomy, aspiration and competence. Psychosomatic well-being is about health complaints such as headaches, stomach aches and musculoskeletal issues. After carefully examining the factors connected to the different dimensions of well-being, the authors highlight the role of autonomy and social support in explaining well-being experiences. They conclude that teleworking is associated with individuals' positive emotions, an increase in job satisfaction and organisational commitment levels, and the amelioration of emotional exhaustion through increased autonomy. When organisational support was present, individuals felt less socially isolated, which, in turn, increased their job satisfaction. They state that social isolation can be mitigated by individual proactivity. In addition, other studies have shown that the relationship between the extent of telework and job satisfaction can be curvilinear, such that satisfaction and amount of telework are positively related at lower levels of telecommuting, but satisfaction plateaus at higher levels of telecommuting (approximately 15.1 hours per week) (Allen et al., 2015). The well-being benefits of part-time telework were also confirmed by Beauregard et al. (2019).

Performance

In their review, Gajendran and Harrison (2007) found that telework positively correlates with *supervisor-rated* and *objectively measured* individual job performance, but not with *self-rated* performance by employees. In the de Menezes and Kelliher (2011) study, measures were based on ratings of managers or employees, with less than a fifth of the studies using an objective measure. Among 42 studies based on ratings, 12 showed a positive relation between telework and individual performance; and in 29 studies, no association was found. It is noteworthy that there were no negative associations. An example of a positive relationship is a study from China. Bloom et al. (2014) report the results of a WFH experiment at a 16 000-employee Chinese travel agency. Call centre employees were randomly assigned to work from home or in the office for nine months. Home working led to a 13 per cent performance increase, of which 9 per cent was from working more minutes per shift (fewer breaks and sick days), and 4 per cent from more calls per minute (attributed to a quieter and more convenient working environment). A systematic review by Mutiganda et al. (2022) investigated the relationship between telework and organisational economic performance indicators such as self-reported employee and organisational performance. They found that self-reported performance was higher for teleworking employees and supervisors than those working in the ordinary workplace. Seven out of 15 studies showed positive benefits of telework on objective organisational performance. Telework was also associated with increased organisational performance, particularly in homogenous samples with unique work tasks.

Multiple locations

Working from multiple locations seems to have its *benefits as well* (Vartiainen and Hyrkkänen, 2010). As seen above, working at home has well-known benefits of autonomy and self-control over time. A main workplace is a place for meetings and dialogues, which are necessary for socialising and creating something new. Moving places such as trains provide an opportunity to interact with interesting strangers and go to exotic locations to work. Travelling also provides chances to be alone, and to think and reflect. 'Secondary workplaces', such as customers' sites and own organisation's satellite offices, are significant places for accomplishing tasks by closely working with clients and communicating with colleagues who otherwise can be difficult to reach. Hotels, cafés, and conference venues, as well as the public areas and lounges of airports as 'third workplaces', are readily available and easy to access. From an employee's viewpoint, feelings of freedom and control over time and schedule may increase in these places. Easy access, on the other hand, may reduce the ability to separate work from one's personal life.

Other benefits

Overall, in addition to autonomy and social support, some *other factors* seem to *moderate* performance and the productivity outcomes of telework (de Menezes and Kelliher, 2011). Golden and Gajendran (2019), in their theoretical framework, proposed that two job characteristics, *job complexity and problem-solving*, and two social characteristics, *interdependence and social support*, moderate the extent of the teleworking–job performance relationship. Testing the issue empirically, they found that teleworkers performing complex and unrelated tasks with low social support had a positive relationship with the extent of telecommuting and performance. This means that the nature of the task matters. Telework has also been associated with better concentration and productivity, as impromptu conversations, and the burdens of social interaction and other distractions at the office, can be avoided (Beauregard et al., 2019; Biron and Van Veldhoven, 2016). Teleworkers lack the distractions of the office and have less involvement in organisational politics; they may be able to schedule their work autonomously and focus on their job tasks more effectively than at the office (Beauregard et al., 2019). Working conditions at home, such as the available physical spaces, ergonomics and the functionality of tools, as well as the composition of the family, naturally affect individual work processes. In some studies, increased productivity from home working has been explained by suggesting that employees merely put in uncounted hours when working from home (Charalampous et al., 2019). The findings also show reduced attrition rates and increased work satisfaction, and no significant impact on performance ratings or promotions, which aligns with earlier studies on low-intensity telework (see, e.g., Beauregard et al., 2019). The study by Choudhury et al. (2022), on the other hand, compared different levels of WFH intensity and found that workers in the intermediate-WFH category reported greater satisfaction with working from home, greater work–life balance, and lower isolation, than workers in the high- and low-WFH categories. The study's findings also suggest that intermediate levels of WFH may result in the enhanced novelty of work products and greater work-related communication.

In their early meta-analysis, Pinsonneault and Boisvert (2001) presented a long and somewhat controversial list of *benefits for organisations*: increased feelings of belonging with the organisation and increased loyalty, retaining best employees, and attracting new ones, increased productivity, decreased rental costs, quicker responsiveness, increased organisational flexibility, and better usage of information systems. Later reviews confirm that generic benefits at the organisational level include lower turnover intent (Beauregard et al., 2019; Gajendran and Harrison, 2007), more opportunities to attract talented employees (Gajendran and Harrison, 2007), less absenteeism (Pinsonneault and Boisvert, 2001; de Menezes and Kelliher, 2011), and financial advantages, for example through decreased real estate costs (Raghuram et al., 2019). Martin and MacDonnell (2012) found telework to increase productivity and retention, strengthen organisational commitment and improve organisational performance. Boell et al. (2013) add increased work morale to the potential benefits, when organisations may benefit from increased job satisfaction among staff. Productivity gains could come because telework may improve the efficiency of organisations in achieving their goals. Improved agility could be realised when telework allows access to work-related information regardless of time and space. Financial advantages can be achieved when organisations can incur cost savings, such as in rent, equipment, and so on. However, findings concerning organisational cost savings are controversial, because the costs are focused elsewhere: teleworkers need ICT infrastructure, adequate ICT security measures in any place they work, ICT staff with the right expertise, and potential training for staff to engage in telework. In addition, increased autonomy for individuals in planning work according to their own pace and productivity cycles impacts upon what organisations need for managing telework, so that teamwork and collaboration can be facilitated and productively performed. That is, as autonomy and flexibility increase for employees, agility and adaptability can decrease for organisations.

Benefits of Working from Home during the Pandemic

Employees' *first reactions* to working from home were *mostly positive* due to the increased autonomy, becoming slightly more critical as forced remote working continued. Ipsen et al.'s (2021) European survey during the early weeks of the pandemic shows that most people had a more positive rather than negative experience of WFH during lockdown; work–life balance, improved perceived work efficiency and greater control over work were considered the main advantages of working from home. One of the potential benefits identified (Schur et al., 2020) was that the pandemic could improve employment opportunities for people with disabilities.

Eurofound (2022) explored some outcomes of telework during the pandemic, using its wide survey data collected from European countries. Overall, employee surveys show that working remotely improved performance and productivity, though negative evidence was also found. Improvements were related to a higher level of education, a good physical environment at home, part-time or hybrid telework, the use of virtual collaboration tools, a goal-based organisation of work and a higher level of trust. Also, employer surveys in six countries report that telework had an overall positive effect on productivity and performance. Evidence also shows that telework improved some aspects of employees' work–life balance, such as scheduling their time with family and doing homework tasks during the pandemic, compared to those working only at their employer's premises. The benefits were strongly related to gender: men have a positive association between work–life balance and telework frequency, and women are best able to balance work and life when they telework occasionally. In general, teleworking employees reported less exposure to physical risks, and therefore their overall physical health was better than those working in non-teleworkable jobs. It seems that occasional forms of telework and hybrid work are associated with higher productivity and better work–life balance, and health and well-being, than full-time telework.

Bloom et al. (2022) performed a randomised control trial that took place in 2021 and 2022 involving 1612 engineers, marketing and finance employees of a large Chinese technology firm. Half of the employees worked from home on Wednesday and Friday, and half worked full-time in the office. There are four key results. First, WFH reduced exhaustion by 35 per cent, and improved self-reported work satisfaction scores. Second, WFH reduced hours worked on home days, but increased it on other work days and weekends, highlighting how home working alters the structure of the working week. Third, WFH employees increased individual messaging and group video call communication, even when in the office, reflecting the impact of remote work on working patterns. Finally, there was no significant impact of WFH on performance ratings or promotions. However, lines of code written increased by 8 per cent, and employees' self-assessed productivity was up 1.8 per cent.

De Vincenzi et al. (2022) reviewed studies concerning the pandemic's *consequences on work organisations* by analysing whether and how the shift towards remote or home working impacted upon the employees' productivity, performance and well-being. Overall, the 67 studies analysed show that remote work per se does not bring positive or negative outcomes, but rather these are consequences of many individual and organisational factors. Individual factors such as employee satisfaction with remote work, ICT tools, COVID-19 countermeasures and digital capability, were related to work productivity and individual performance. Some individual factors positively impacted upon well-being, such as proactive coping strategies – that is, help-seeking and active problem-focused coping – as well as recreation and relaxation activities to cope with work-related stress. Some personality traits were related to personal well-being, such as low levels of solitude and neuroticism, high levels of extraversion and agreeableness, and moderate levels of conscientiousness and openness. Workers who considered themselves self-disciplined claimed to be more able to deal positively with the work–family balance. In addition, self-compassion also emerged as a competence that promotes employees' well-being. In line with this, mindfulness was positively related to job satisfaction and negatively associated with technostress. Similarly, emotional intelligence was also shown to reduce the negative impact of social isolation on employees' well-being.

Organisational and workplace factors provide resources to employees to create a proper work environment at home and elsewhere, and technical support and training enhance productivity. In a similar vein, leaders offering digital support and avoiding intrusive monitoring positively influenced employees' performance. Employees can also craft their use of technologies: for example, switching off notifications, powering off electronic devices at a specific time in the evening, or responding to emails only at a predefined time. Quality in interpersonal relationships among colleagues and managers has also proven to bring positive effects. Co-workers' support was linked to a lower workload perception and a more positive work–home balance. Leaders can promote and sustain organisational and social support, increasing the perception of psychological safety among teleworkers. In terms of more general management, a study showed the relevance of organisational communication for positive outcomes.

However, studies regarding the *impacts* of remote and telework from home during the pandemic are also *controversial*. Shirmohammadi et al. (2022) analysed 40 recent empirical studies published on work–life balance during the COVID-19 pandemic between March 2020 and August 2021. They found four tensions representing misfits between desirable expectations and the undesirable realities of remote work. First, one of the advantages of remote work discussed is the temporal flexibility. However, the pandemic-induced research suggests that remote work was also accompanied by work intensification, for example working late in the evenings. Second, locational flexibility is the key feature of traditional remote and telework. However, during the pandemic, space limitations became a challenge for many remote workers, who missed adequate physical space and had to work at home. Third, using ICTs makes remote work and collaboration possible. However, research conducted during the pandemic highlighted technostress and isolation as two major challenges that employees working from home confronted while depending on ICTs to work. Adjusting to the use of ICTs and the complexity of platforms increased the psychological burdens employees experienced, especially for those who worked from home for the first time, felt unprepared, or lacked the appropriate technological tools. Fourth, family-friendly work arrangement has been viewed as the possibility to take care of family members, integrate work and family roles, and offer means for employees to adjust their work schedules to meet household needs and care responsibilities. However, in practice, it was challenging to mix work and family roles.

EXPECTED BENEFITS AND OPPORTUNITIES OF HYBRID WORK IN EUROPE

The expectations regarding the benefits and opportunities of HW on the individual, team, organisation and society levels are shown and discussed next. This is done by analysing the content of country reports and linked reports concerning the benefit and opportunity expectations of the various actors, including social partners, managers and the media. As expected, there were many similarities with the earlier studies. The following questions are answered: What benefits were expected from hybrid work after the pandemic, and what opportunities are there to realise them?

Opportunities are discussed more broadly in Chapter 7, which focuses on the success factors in implementing telework and hybrid work arrangements. Identifying opportunities as resources for telework requires the identification of hindrances and challenges, the removal of hindrances, and then overcoming challenges by developing practices, guidelines and principles when designing and implementing telework. The resources include the principles, and managerial and human resources (HR) practices, needed to develop and sustain teleworking arrangements, communication practices related to collaboration with particular attention to specific cultural features, and technologies and tools available to support telework.

Analysis

The benefits and opportunities were analysed, first identifying their type and content, after which the levels of impact – that is, employee (workers, superiors), organisation (management, owner) and society – were coded using the definitions listed below:

- *Benefits:* the kinds of benefits implementing home working (HW) arrangements could offer as resources for individuals, teams, organisations, and so on.
- *Opportunities (enablers):* the kinds of opportunities some features of successful HW can offer to avoid or remove hindrances and overcome challenges.
- *Level of impact:* who is impacted upon by the implementation of HW: individuals (employees, superiors), teams, organisations (management) and society.

Findings

In all, 97 citations concerning expected *benefits* (N = 97) in hybrid work appeared in the data, especially at the individual level (Table 6.1). Although maintaining work–life balance was seen as both a hindrance and a challenge, it was also considered a benefit due to increased autonomy, and because it also possibly increased the health and well-being of individual employees. The ability to balance work and family life, and reduced management control, seemed to be particularly important. Time and cost savings from reduced commuting, and observations about increased efficiency and productivity when working from home, were other expected individual-level benefits of hybrid work. In addition, motivational and creativity-related benefits were mentioned. On the organisational level, cost savings, especially due to reduced office space needs, and opportunities to recruit new workers, new practices, and productivity increases, were commonly expected benefits. At the societal level, the identified benefits were related to sustainability issues such as reduced commuting, avoiding traffic jams, and saving time for employees.

Opportunities (N = 126) include practices, guidelines and principles identified as important resources when implementing hybrid work. This reflected an orientation of preparation for the post-pandemic period. From the individual perspective, it was considered important to concentrate efforts on developing leadership practices and working guidelines, working conditions, and ICT as enablers of hybrid work; agreements on work arrangements, for example, costs, training new competencies, and increasing autonomy and flexibility. Most of the expected opportunities, however, were related to the organisational level.

Table 6.1 The topics and number of expected benefits and opportunities in hybrid work on the individual, team, organisation and societal levels

BENEFITS (N = 97)	OPPORTUNITIES (N = 126)
Employees (workers, superiors)	
Work–life balance (N = 13), autonomy (N = 8), reduced commuting (N = 7), efficiency (N = 5), costs (N = 4), health and well-being (N = 3), motivation (N = 3), productivity (N = 3), working conditions (N = 3), creativity (N = 2), knowledge (N = 2), leadership (N = 2), other: career, equality, flexibility, job satisfaction, leisure, recruitment, safety, social relations, trust, working location, workload	Leadership (N = 5), working conditions (N = 4), ICT (N = 4), HW agreements (N = 3), training (N = 3), autonomy (N = 2), costs (N = 2), flexibility (N = 2), guidelines (N = 2), other: work–life balance, physical activity, monitoring, employment relationship, data security
Team	
Self-leadership	HW agreements
Organisation (management viewpoint)	
Costs (N = 12), recruitment (N = 5), productivity (N = 4), learning (N = 2), other: working location, new business	HW agreements (N = 13), ICT (N = 10), office (N = 9), leadership (N = 7), training (N = 6), communication (N = 5), costs (N = 3), health and well-being (N = 3), recruitment (N = 3), guidelines (N = 2), HR (N = 2), other: concentration, competence, control, employment relationship, participation, working conditions, work culture, working location
Society	
Commuting (N = 4), other: working location	Legislation (N = 5), HW agreements (N = 4), tax (N = 3), other: training, working conditions, working location, recruitment, ICT, data security

Source: Vartiainen and Vanharanta (2023, pp. 49–50).

From the *perspective of organisations*, hybrid work was expected to provide an opportunity (but also a requirement), among other elements, to reconsider and redesign types of work contracts, digitalise work processes and procedures by diversifying ICT use, develop office spaces to better meet the needs of hybrid employees, and develop human resources (HR) and managerial practices and guidelines. The need for new competencies requires training, and collaboration requires communication. The perceived *societal-level* opportunities were mostly related to the need to develop and change labour legislation, collective agreements and taxation to incentivise remote work. It is worth noting that, in practice, there were no opportunities to develop team-level issues identified.

BENEFITS AS DESIGN FEATURES AND OPPORTUNITIES FOR HOW TO USE THEM IN HYBRID WORK

Benefits and related expectations of hybrid work are important driving forces to implement hybrid work. In addition, they can be used as the design criteria. The question is whether the individual benefit expectations can be fitted with the organisational benefits. If they are agreed upon, they can be used to formulate common goals and practices. The key benefits and opportunities on different levels (I = individual, T = team, O = organisation, S = society) in the remote work and telework literature and country reports are summarised in Figure 6.1.

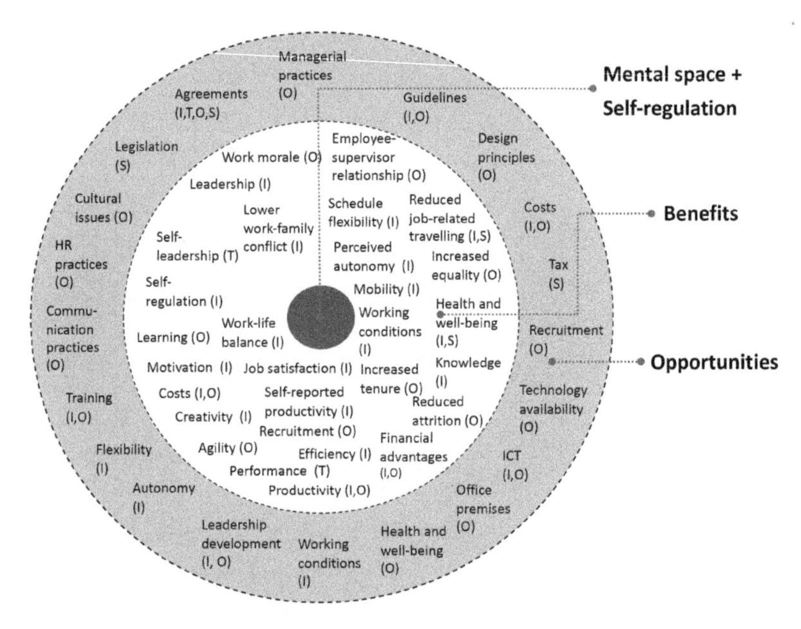

Source: Modified from Vartiainen and Vanharanta (2023, p. 52).

Figure 6.1 *Summary of benefits and opportunities on different levels (I = individual, T = team, O = organisation, S = society) in the remote work and telework literature and country reports on expectations regarding hybrid work in Europe*

From Hindrances and Challenges to Benefits in Hybrid Work

In all, the evidence from the traditional remote and telework *literature on expected benefits is somewhat controversial.* The analysis of the review articles shows that telework research has primarily focused on individual-level outcomes (Raghuram et al., 2019). In addition, the findings are sometimes ambivalent, contradictory and varied, and often lack consistent evidence. This is explained by the different contexts in which telework has been studied, and the multitude of moderating factors that influence the outcomes (e.g., de Menezes and Kelliher, 2011). Some benefits have a curvilinear relationship with telework intensity, whereas some challenges and benefits are accentuated as the intensity of telework increases. Studies also show some positive implications of telework levelling off as the intensity of telework increases. For example, Biron and Van Veldhoven (2016) show how increases in job satisfaction drop off as teleworking becomes more extensive. The same phenomenon has been found in relation to autonomy. Gajendran and Harrison's (2007) meta-analysis shows how both high- and low-intensity telecommuters experience similar levels of autonomy, which suggests that after an initial increase in the perception of autonomy accruing from 1–2 days of telework, there is only a marginal increase in feelings of autonomy as time spent telecommuting increases.

The *benefits* discussed in the telework literature and expectations regarding HW during the pandemic were very similar at the individual, organisational and societal levels. At the *individual level*, although keeping work and life in balance was seen as both a hindrance and a challenge, it was also considered a benefit due to increased autonomy, and because it could also improve the health and well-being of individual employees. Time and cost savings from the reduced amount of commuting, and increased efficiency and productivity when working from home, are other expected individual-level benefits of hybrid work. However, more evidence is needed for these savings to be proven realistic. At the *organisational level*, cost savings, especially due to the reduced need for office space, as well as opportunities to recruit new workers, the development of new practices, flexibility, and productivity increases, were commonly expected benefits. At the *societal level*, the identified benefits are related to sustainability issues such as reduced commutes, fewer traffic jams and employee time savings. The telework literature also discusses the inclusion of disabled people as a societal benefit of telework, but this was not discussed as a HW expectation in the reports reviewed in this study.

Regarding *opportunities*, which refer to the practices, guidelines and principles identified as important resources when implementing telework, the telework literature and the HW expectations highlight the importance of developing supportive leadership and HR practices, and providing working guidelines and technologies for the successful implementation of these work arrangements. The telework literature and HW discussions both address the need to develop an organisational culture and communication patterns that are supportive of telework. What is highlighted in the HW expectations and not discussed in the telework literature is the need for agreements on work arrangements and the redesigning of work contracts, as well as, at a more macro level, changes to labour legislation and collective agreements. Office spaces must be developed to better meet the needs of hybrid employees who may use them only occasionally, and in addition, to attract them to come to the office when needed.

During the pandemic in 2020–22, many local, national and global surveys were conducted concerning the expectations of both employees and management about the post-pandemic hybrid work outlook. In a global survey (Strack et al., 2021) in late 2020, nine out of ten respondents said that they wanted to work remotely at least some of the time, and only a small proportion of workers – one in four – would switch to a completely remote model if they could. This refers to the desire to organise work individually and team-wise. This wish for continuing remote work and telework options was not limited to those with digital, knowledge or office jobs, but included social care, services and manufacturing. In regard to temporal flexibility, 36 per cent of respondents wanted a traditional 9-to-5 job with fully fixed hours, 44 per cent would prefer a combination of fixed and flexible time, and 20 per cent would like to have complete time flexibility. In a survey by Microsoft[1] in early 2022, the number of people engaging in hybrid work was up by 7 per cent year-over-year (to 38 per cent); and over half of the respondents (52 per cent), especially Gen Z and Millennials, said that they were likely to consider shifting to hybrid or remote work in the year ahead. From an organisational viewpoint, this may result in challenges if not properly considered. A survey conducted by McKinsey suggests that most organisations also saw value in hybrid work, and planned to combine remote and on-site working after the pandemic (Alexander et al., 2021). Most executives expected that employees would be on site between 21 and 80 per cent of the time, or one to four days per week.

The key principles in terms of future job design are, on the one hand, to remove hindrances or change the above-mentioned challenges; on the other hand, to utilise and develop the available benefits as targets, and opportunities as resources. The post-pandemic hybrid work type will determine what resources are needed to address the situation in hand. It seems evident that hybrid work will be a flexible mixture of using various spaces – including the home and main office – as digitalised workplaces.

NOTE

1. The Work Trend Index survey was conducted by an independent research firm, Edelman Data x Intelligence, among 31 102 full-time employed or self-employed workers across 31 countries, between 7 January 2022 and 16 February 2022.

7. Design, implementation, adjustment, and crafting hybrid work

Make hybrid work

What makes hybrid work work? It very much depends on how the design and implementation processes are realised. The next question is: What is successful hybrid work? It is defined here as achieving the organisational outcomes and goals and the well-being and job satisfaction of the hybrid workers. Gohoungodji et al. (2023) looked for factors that affect telework implementation and its success in a systematic literature review of 83 articles covering empirical evidence from 2000 to 2021. They categorised *success factors* into two groups: factors related to teleworkers, and factors related to a teleworker's environment. Factors related to a teleworker are personal resources such as experience, skills and personal characteristics. Factors related to the environment are categorised into three groups: materials and conditions, work environment, and teleworker family environment. Materials and conditions include adequate data-secured information and communication technologies, and the physical environment in workplaces. Work environment includes social relations with management, superiors and co-workers. And family environment includes issues such as family–work facilitation, and workspaces at home. By comparing success factors, researchers identified dominant factors having an overall impact on the effectiveness of telework: media richness, experience, communication, work–family facilitation, supervisor support, technological support, top management support, motivation, technology mastery and trust. They are crucial for the successful implementation of telework, as they all have a dominant and positive overall effect. It is underlined that success factors seem to change over time, and influence either the telework success directly, or other factors indirectly which in turn impact on the success of telework.

This chapter shows, first, what is known about *success factors in implementing* remote and telework. Research on telework has proposed several factors underlying the successful implementation of working from home, including planning, managerial approaches and human resource management (HRM) practices, characteristics of organisational culture that support telework, and required tools and technologies. It is expected that although hybrid work can differ in form from earlier remote work and telework, it can benefit from prior implementation experiences with such work arrangements. The transformation to a hybrid work mode is a process that starts by considering its purpose and ends by evaluating the outcomes. The transformation consists of designing, implementing, adjusting and crafting sub-processes. The remote work literature and the expectations for home working (HW) in organisations during the pandemic emphasise the importance of developing management and human resources (HR) practices and providing working instructions and sufficient technologies to implement these work arrangements successfully. Theory and empirical-based discussions both bring up the need to put more effort into developing an organisational culture and communication patterns supportive of telework. What was highlighted in HW expectations during the pandemic, but not discussed in the telework literature, is the need for agreements regarding work arrangements and the redesigning of work contracts in organisations. In addition, changes in labour legislation and collective agreements could facilitate the identification of balanced forms and implementations of hybrid work arrangements. The development and renewal of office spaces to foster community, and support creative and innovative interactions, could be an opportunity to attract employees back to the office. It also seems that when recruiting new – young – employees, offering a hybrid work option would be an attractive factor in every way. In all, the implementation should support the hybridisation process schematically illustrated in Figure 3.2 in Chapter 3.

FACTORS TO IMPACT DURING THE HYBRID WORK TRANSFORMATION

The Role of Goals, Context, Resources and Design Elements

The most important things to pay attention to when designing and implementing hybrid work are the goal of an organisation and the needs of employees. The main benefits expected by employers are agility, effectiveness and cost savings; while employees expect more autonomy, well-being, and maintenance of work–life balance, as shown in Chapter 6. As not all tasks are suitable for telework, the nature of work and its components are important to recognise. The purpose of an organisation, that is, its goals and individual needs satisfaction, affect what demand characteristics in the work environment and what kind of resources are needed by those making changes. They also influence what kinds of constituent elements, sub-elements, and current and potential features are reasonable to use to configure a hybrid work unit. The outcomes of working processes are dependent on these factors. Figure 7.1 shows the main factors influencing the configuration of a hybrid work unit.

There are many opportunities to develop hybrid work in a sustainable manner, considering both the well-being and engagement of employees, and

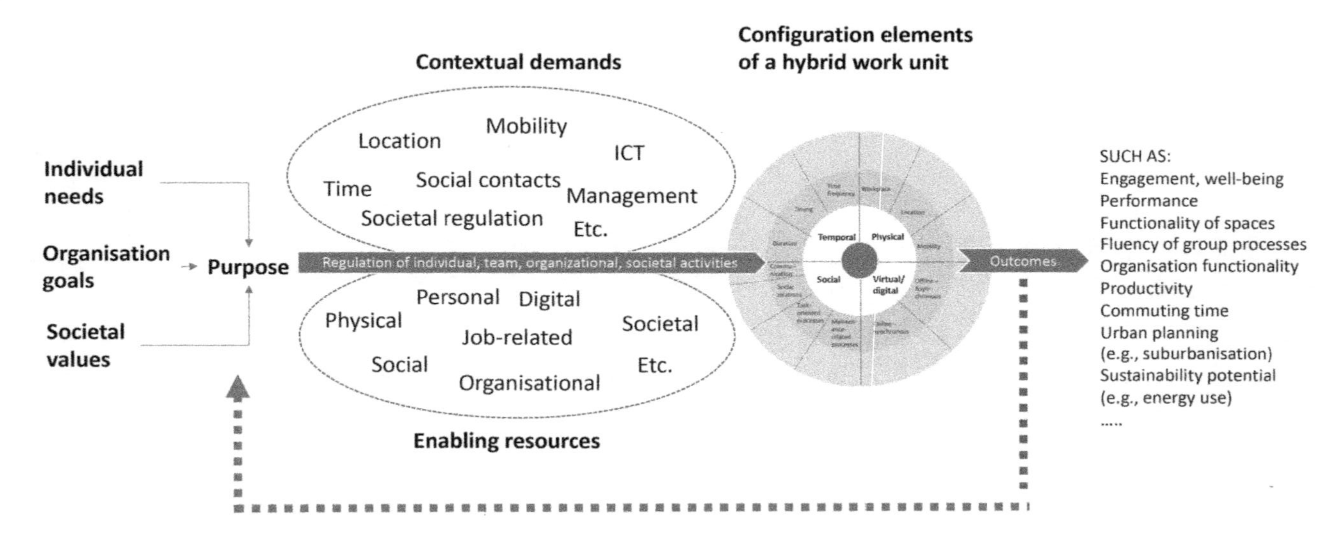

Figure 7.1 *The successful configuration of a hybrid work unit requires focusing on organisational goals and individual needs as well as on the compatibility of contextual job demands and available resources to achieve expected outcomes*

their performance and flexibility expectations in organisations. These opportunities are based on the advantages of remote work and telework in general, and the expected benefits of hybrid work that were discussed in Chapter 6. It is also possible to transform challenging work demands into opportunities by using individual and collective resources in this transformation. Working from home (WFH) during the COVID-19 pandemic strengthened some factors already apparent in earlier remote work and telework literature; however, it also revealed some new features to focus upon. How, and in which order, design, implementation and working in hybrid work mode finally happens depends on an organisation's culture and values, decision-making traditions and present practices. This implies that the design and implementation can start from the expected outcome features, for example by aiming to identify the best hybrid work composition to ensure the effectiveness and well-being of employees.

Hybridisability of Work

The starting point is to identify the *organisation's readiness for change.* Assessing the organisational environment, and organisational and job suitability for telework, and establishing telework policies and agreements, are fundamental for the successful implementation of telework (Bernardino et al., 2012; Overmyer, 2011; Pyöriä, 2011). The assessment of the external environment entails understanding the requirements outlined in labour legislation, possible agreements between social partners, and how they will be implemented in the organisation. The assessment of the internal environment concerns the analysis of fit among different occupations, task descriptions, individual characteristics and preferences for telework (Overmyer, 2011; Pyöriä, 2011). A telework agreement between an employee and the organisation outlines the specific work arrangement agreed upon by both parties (Overmyer, 2011).

Next is to identify *what jobs and tasks can be hybridised, what are their contextual demands, and what resources are available.* In principle, the hybrid work concept offers almost limitless alternatives ('Hybrid is something that is formed by combining two or more things') to configure work elements and features. However, the reality of working life shows that typically hybrid work consists of flexible use of different locations, time and technologies, that is, hybrid telework. For the breakdown of hybridity potential in an organisation, it is important to understand that jobs are bundles of tasks and units of work activities, with the help of which individuals and groups using tools produce outcomes. Work activities also require human and social resources, such as skills and competencies that enable working in a specific context. Therefore, determining the hybridisability of any individual and team-level jobs requires analysing their content, and the tools and resources needed to meet the requirements. Some tasks cannot be performed remotely outside the main office, given current production processes.

Teleworkability – although not hybridisability – of jobs and occupations for working from home has been analysed before and during the pandemic. The International Labour Organization (ILO, 2021a) estimated the potential for working from home across the globe before the pandemic, and found that close to 18 per cent of workers worked in occupations and lived in countries with the infrastructure that would have allowed them to effectively perform their work from home. The probability of working from home was between zero and 2 per cent in occupations such as plant and machine operator and assembler, or service and sales worker, whereas among managers and professionals, half of them could potentially work from home. From the design viewpoint, by access to broadband Internet and the likelihood of owning a personal computer, the housing situation allowing working from home, or whether the person has the necessary social networks, such as having fixed clients, for other types of home-based work, must be considered. There are large differences between countries. For example, Delaporte and Peña (2020) estimated that the share of jobs which can be performed at home in 23 Latin American and Caribbean (LAC) countries varied from 7 per cent in Guatemala to 16 per cent in the Bahamas. Dingel and Neiman (2020) found that 37 per cent of jobs in the United States could be performed entirely at home, with significant variation across cities, industries and professions.

In Europe, Sostero et al. (2020) gave an estimation that 37 per cent of dependent employment in the European Union (EU) was teleworkable in 2018. The portion of teleworkable employment ranged between 33 per cent and 44 per cent because of differences in employment structures. Sostero et al. (2020) calculated that telework uptake varied in the EU between 45 per cent for teachers and information and communication technology (ICT) professionals, and less than 10 per cent for sales and service workers. Two indexes were used in the analysis. The technical teleworkability index is based on the presence of physical tasks, and the social interaction index further qualifies jobs that are technically teleworkable but might benefit from on-site presence. The indexes are based on a conceptual framework and taxonomy of tasks for occupational analysis by Fernández-Macías and Bisello (2020). The framework covers three elements of jobs. First, the 'task contents' of work can be physical, intellectual and social interaction tasks. Second, the 'methods of work' refer to forms of work organisation in performing the tasks, that is, how autonomous or controlled work is; whether teamwork is performed; and whether work is routine or creative. And third, the 'tools of work' refer to the type of technology in use. These kinds of elements could be used before the transformation to evaluate the potential to implement hybrid telework by profiling different jobs.

According to Sostero et al. (2020), even starker differences in teleworkability emerge between high-income and low-income workers, between white- and blue-collar workers, and among genders. However, the enforced closure of workplaces during the pandemic also resulted in many new teleworkers among low- and mid-level clerical and administrative workers with limited access to such arrangements. Dingel and Neiman (2020) found that 37 per cent of jobs in the United States can also be performed entirely at home, with significant variation across occupations. Managers and those working with computers, in finance and law, can primarily work from home. In contrast, frontline employees such as health care practitioners and cleaning, construction and production workers, cannot. Those who can work from home typically earn more. This divide is familiar, as the review by Bailey and Kurland (2002) mentioned.

Contextual Demands

The transformation to hybrid work means changes in the working environments. These changes create new job demands that require appropriate resources to adapt. From the design viewpoint, the expected hindrances in work should be avoided, and challenges should be influenced, compensated for and strategically navigated. The expected benefits and opportunities play the role of potential resources for designing, implementing and carrying out hybrid work. The crucial questions for designing and implementing hybrid work are about what kinds of constituent elements, sub-elements, and current and potential features are under consideration, as well as the kinds of resources that are available for an operating subject – be it an individual, a team, the management of an organisation, their network or a society – to adapt, use, benefit from and develop. Work demands in hybrid work are objective, determinable elements and features of work and the working context. For example, location flexibility can allow high mobility if needed, and time flexibility can offer the possibility of scheduling work autonomously within certain limits. However, demands can also create some hindrances and challenges if actors do not have enough resources to meet them. Demands can also become benefits and developmental opportunities for actors when additional resources are granted.

Available Resources

Demands are met with resources. Work as a systemic entity provides many kinds of resources to both an organisation and an individual. These resources are used dynamically to meet the changing demands of work. The job demands–resources (JD-R) model (Demerouti et al., 2001; Bakker and Demerouti, 2017) states that job resources needed to meet the hindrances and challenges in the working context can be found in the very same physical, virtual, social and organisational aspects of work that create hindrances and challenges. In addition, personal resources such as skills and competencies help in adjusting to changes in work. The model suggests the need to reduce job demands, and the associated physiological and psychological costs, to stimulate personal growth, learning and development. *Job-related resources* are the physical, social, organisational, or other aspects of work that reduce hindering and challenging job demands and the associated costs (Schaufeli and Bakker, 2004). For example, it is expected that in hybrid work, the usefulness and functionality of digital tools and proper working conditions at any location act as virtual and physical resources, and colleagues and leaders at the workplace, and family and friends at home and elsewhere, act as social resources by providing support, help and appreciation.

In addition to the contextual resources, hybrid working employees can rely on their own *personal resources*. These refer to positive self-evaluations and competencies of remote workers and teleworkers that manifest as proactivity and an individual's sense of their ability to successfully control and impact upon their environment (Hobfoll et al., 2018). For example, prior experiences and learned practices involving telework increased personal resources in working from home during the pandemic. Specific individual characteristics, capabilities and competencies have been proposed as particularly suitable for teleworking, such as self-management skills, the ability to communicate efficiently by using technologies, and the ability to navigate cultural diversity (Blackburn et al., 2003).

Peiró and Martínez-Tur (2022) identify three clusters of competencies needed now and in the future: *non-digital, digital and digitalised competencies*. Examples of non-digital competencies are adaptability, entrepreneurship, creativity, critical thinking, readiness to learn, and communication and collaboration skills. Non-digital competences are still needed, because relevant tasks that require social or relational skills will continue to exist (for example, negotiation processes, selling, and so on). Non-digital competencies can evolve into digitalised competencies. This is a pervasive phenomenon based on the digitalisation and transformation of jobs and professions. Digital competencies refer to the skills listed in the European Digital Competence Framework for Citizens (DigiComp), such as information and data literacy, and digital communication and collaboration. Peiró and Martínez-Tur (2022, p. 192) define digitalised competencies as 'as non-digital competences that, when carried out in digital contexts (e.g., telework or virtual teamwork) and/or in cooperation with digital devices or "actors" (e.g., cobots, or artificial intelligence algorithms), are deeply transformed in order to be effective'. This transformation often affects the components of the competence: knowledge, skills, attitudes, and the necessary behaviours to enact the competence in the new context. It is important to develop policies to train people in these digitalised competences.

One challenge can be that not all employees who are skilled at their jobs are in teleworkable jobs, and teleworking employees may not have the necessary skills. The telework literature suggests that these characteristics and competencies should be considered when recruiting personnel for positions in which teleworking is possible and encouraged (Bernardino et al., 2012; Offstein et al., 2010). Training in remote work practices and technologies has also been identified as one of the HRM success factors in telework (Greer and Payne, 2014; Kurland and Cooper, 2002; Martínez-Sánchez et al., 2008; Pérez et al., 2005). Relatedly, the successful implementation of telework sets requirements for technologies and data security that need to be addressed when planning, budgeting and training for work outside an organisation's premises (Overmyer, 2011).

Basic Elements and Sub-elements in Work Design

The main adjustable elements and sub-elements of a hybrid work system are based on the interplay of the four basic space elements answering design questions concerning where to work, with what tools and with whom, and when, for how long and how often.

For example, location, workplace and mobility are the sub-elements of physical space. Various workplaces in different locations in neighbourhoods, urban and rural areas, in different parts of the country, in other countries, and across the globe can be used as working locations. The features of the workplace in each location, as physical premises and working environments, vary according to the needs of the organisation and its employees. Mobility brings with it contextual changes in both location and workplace; a hybrid worker becomes multilocational.

Virtual space allows the use of various tools and software to seek information and knowledge, communicate and collaborate synchronously and asynchronously with others if needed, and do remote solo work by searching for information and knowledge in virtual spaces.

The sub-elements of social space include communication and social relation-related arrangements between actors – that is, colleagues, management, superiors, customers, family members and friends – to guarantee fluent task and maintenance-related group processes face-to-face, virtually or in a mixed manner, online and offline.

The temporal element includes time-related sub-elements, which are needed to decide when, for how long and how often work is done, and considering timewise changes in the working environment and available resources.

TRANSFORMATION EXPERIENCES IN REMOTE AND TELEWORK

The transformation process towards hybrid work should be a collaborative project between management and employees. *Implementation* as a process means installing and configuring a hybrid work solution, and training staff on how to work effectively and in a sustainable manner from the perspective of their well-being. *Adoption* means having the entire organisation embrace that new solution, wrap it into their workflow, and become more effective and sustainable socially. This requires the participation of all personnel in the change project, which helps to adjust and cope with changes. *Adjustment* to hybrid work can be defined as an employee's ability to adapt to multiple locations, virtual work modes, flexible social relations and timings when moving from typical office surroundings to hybrid work. Employee *job crafting* offers ways to improve the functionality of the hybrid work solution after gaining experience from it.

Implementation

Organisational factors facilitating the implementation of remote and telework are shown in Table 7.1. The pro-telework organisational culture is a prerequisite to enable the design or redesign of new flexible forms of organising. Even if organisations have flexible work policies, the *organisational culture* may still discourage employees from working remotely if physical presence is considered a sign of productivity (Gonsalves, 2020) and if remote work is perceived as risky from the perspective of career advancement (Mello, 2007). Therefore, organisational culture significantly influences employees' willingness to telework (Mello, 2007). Specific cultural characteristics such as trust (Offstein et al., 2010), a culture that supports change and innovation (Pérez et al., 2005) and a culture that recognises the legitimacy of remote work (Gonsalves, 2020; Greer and Payne, 2014) have been identified as important cultural characteristics supporting the adoption of telework.

Managerial approaches are critical in creating a sense that telework is valued equally to work on company premises. The top leaders' attitudes matter. For example, a Spanish study (Mayo et al., 2016) with a sample of 2388 top managers showed that a company's teleworking offer is more common when these key decision-makers believe in the importance of work–family balance. Earlier research on remote and telework highlights the need to focus on performance-based evaluation as opposed to presence-based evaluation (Bernardino et al., 2012; Martínez-Sánchez et al., 2007a; Overmyer, 2011).

This requires the establishment of clear performance objectives and measures for both employees and managers (Illegems and Verbeke, 2004).

New *human resources* management practices are needed, as the management needs to be attentive to the equal treatment of individuals working remotely and those working on company premises (Morganson et al., 2010). Telework also requires additional effort from management to establish and maintain social ties within the team (Offstein et al., 2010) and the willingness and skills to engage in the remote monitoring, mentoring, and managing of employees (Kurland and Cooper, 2002; Pérez et al., 2005). Rich communication, which can be achieved using different forms of communication, is central to strengthening employee commitment to the organisation and maintaining trustful relationships between managers and employees (Offstein et al., 2010). Tools and technologies are necessary in both communication and searching for information and knowledge.

Adjustment

Adjustment refers to the act of adapting to a particular condition, position or purpose of work. On the individual level, adapting refers to performing adaptive actions that address changing conditions. Adjustment to online work has been defined as an employee's ability to adapt to virtual work modes when moving from typical office surroundings to remote work (van Zoonen et al., 2021). While autonomy to adjust the time and place, as well as deciding on work practices according to personal needs and preferences, are inarguably the central advantages of remote and telework from the individual perspective, studies emphasise the importance of having clear structures and guidelines provided by management; for example, in the formation of well-functioning collaboration practices (Bartsch et al., 2020). The need for clarity and guidelines was also reflected by van Zoonen et al. (2021), who found that employees who reported higher levels of independence and clarity of job instructions were better able to adjust to remote work than other employees. Thus, to facilitate individual telework, organisations should ensure clear objectives and goals, and minimise task interdependencies among organisational members where possible. This concerns individual, solo work. The other side of the coin is that decreasing the interdependency of the group members in completing their tasks can lead to social isolation. This in turn could open the way to feelings of loneliness. Therefore, when the interdependency of tasks is high, developing collaboration practices, support and tools is necessary.

In addition to increased autonomy, other factors positively impact upon adjustment. In an early study on teleworking (Peters et al., 2001), the number of business localities, high level of education and information technology (IT) skills, small children at home, and longer than a one-hour one-way

Table 7.1 *Organisational factors facilitating the successful implementation of telework*

DOMAINS	SUPPORTING FACTORS
Organisational culture	• Pro-telework culture (Greer and Payne, 2014) • Culture that supports innovation and change (Pérez et al., 2005) • Culture of trust (Offstein et al., 2010) • Culture that emphasises interpersonal relationships and societal values (Strack et al., 2021) • Organisational culture and practices that focus on well-being and appreciate boundary setting (Gascoigne, 2021) • Office space that signals flexibility (Gonsalves, 2020)
Design	• Analysis of the external environment and labour laws (Bernardino et al., 2012; Pyöriä, 2011) • Analysis of the internal environment (Bernardino et al., 2012) • Telework strategy (Overmyer, 2011) • Written telework policies and telework agreements (Beauregard et al., 2013; Overmyer, 2011; Pyöriä, 2011)
Management approach	• Evaluation based on performance (Bernardino et al., 2012; Martínez-Sánchez et al., 2007a; Overmyer, 2011) • Results orientation (Offstein et al., 2010) • Proactive and inclusive management style (Overmyer, 2011) • Promoting both enabling and managing leadership styles (Bartsch et al., 2020) • Decentralised decision-making and middle managers' willingness to monitor remotely jobs suitable for teleworking (Pérez et al., 2005) • Effective remote mentoring and management (Kurland and Cooper, 2002) • Clear performance objectives and measures for employees and managers (Illegems and Verbeke, 2004; Mello, 2007) • The use of a variety of forms of communication (Offstein et al., 2010) • Creation of social ties and bonds within team (Offstein et al., 2010) • Balancing governance with flexibility (Strack et al., 2021)
Communication practices	• Forums and tools for informal interaction accessible to telecommuters and non-telecommuters (Kurland and Cooper, 2002; Shirmohammadi et al., 2022; Strack et al., 2021) • Reduction of social isolation through synchronous video meetings and informal communication (van Zoonen et al., 2021)

DOMAINS	SUPPORTING FACTORS
Tools and technologies	• Including telework technologies in budgets (Overmyer, 2011) • Access to technological tools that support telework (Golden and Raghuram, 2010; Mello, 2007; Strack et al., 2021) • Focus on security issues while implementing telework policies (Overmyer, 2011) • Ergonomic and distraction-free workspace at home (Akuoko et al., 2021; Beauregard et al., 2013; Carillo et al., 2021; Mello, 2007)
HRM practices	• Decentralisation of HRM practices (Bernardino et al., 2012) • Recruiting individuals with teleworking capabilities (Bernardino et al., 2012; Offstein et al., 2010) • HR commitment practices (Martínez-Sánchez et al., 2008) • Training management to supervise telework (Gascoigne, 2021; McCarthy et al., 2020) • Telework training (Bernardino et al., 2012) • Training in ICT use and remote work practices (Greer and Payne, 2014; Kurland and Cooper, 2002; Martínez-Sánchez et al., 2008; Pérez et al., 2005; Shirmohammadi et al., 2022) • Holistic approach to employee well-being (Strack et al., 2021) • Offering a range of remote work options (Shirmohammadi et al., 2022) • Ensuring access to development opportunities and mentoring (Gascoigne, 2021) • Experimentation and monitoring of HW practices (Strack et al., 2021)

Source: Modified from Vartiainen and Vanharanta (2023, pp. 55–56).

commuting time, were positively related to telework adoption. The quality of telework technology, that is, higher social richness and telepresence, leads to higher telework motivation (Venkatesh and Johnson, 2002). The teleworker's self-efficacy is positively related to employees' adjustment, especially among those employees who telework more extensively (Raghuram et al., 2003). A survey study of 156 Spanish firms (Martínez-Sánchez et al., 2007b) indicated that HR development practices are positively associated with the intensity of telework adoption, and they moderate the relationship between telework and firm performance.

The visible part of organisational culture (Schein, 1990), the physical environment, may also influence employee attitudes towards flexibility. In a recent study, Gonsalves (2020) found that changing from a traditional office setting to a multi-space office[1] increased employees' willingness to work remotely. Without assigned desks in the office, the physical environment signalled flexibility, and an individual's presence, or absence, was not monitored, which encouraged them to be more flexible in terms of the physical location where their work took place. For example, ensuring an adequate workspace at home (good ergonomics, free from distraction and noise) was identified as a key to employees' successful adjustment to remote work, in addition to work–life balance, during the pandemic (Akuoko et al., 2021; Carillo et al., 2021).

Resistance and Risks

The implementation of hybrid work is also resisted for *different reasons*. Pyöriä (2011) names a few. An established contractual framework and culture of teleworking can be absent in an organisation. Telework may not suit everyone, because of their job content, or because it does not fit with their life situation, for example, there are small children in a small apartment. In addition, social relations in the workplace (including customer contacts) can be considered more important than the flexibility afforded by telework. In the traditional management culture, managers can resist change because they are reluctant to relinquish their power. The paternalistic management style strengthens differences in managerial and employee perspectives regarding the major restructuring of HR practices, including the appraisal mechanism, work environment, social isolation, work–life (im)balance, technological difficulties, workplace monitoring, retrenchment and work contracts, as observed during the pandemic in India (Ganguly et al., 2022).

Job Crafting

A question is: Who designs and develops? It can happen top-down, bottom-up or between them as a dialogical process. A designer can be management, a professional from inside an organisation, or an external expert. The personnel play a crucial role as they finally accept, or resist and reject, the change proposals. An ongoing way to design and influence work by employees during the implementation and after it is job crafting. *Job crafting* refers to proactive behaviour where employees customise their job demands and resources, and adjust their working practices and work environment to suit their tasks and individual preferences (Hyrkkänen et al., 2022). Based on the JD-R model (Demerouti et al., 2001; Bakker and Demerouti, 2017), the resource-based perspective explains job crafting as individuals' efforts to change their jobs in order to increase resources and reduce hindrance, and challenge demands to minimise the person–job misfit (Tims et al., 2012). Employees engage in job crafting to change what is required of them in their work by managing resources, and thus making work more meaningful, engaging, satisfying and productive.

The transformation to hybrid work leads to new work-related demands arising from expanding the operational environments, that is, spaces of work. Typically, the changes concern the places where to work, and scheduling when to work. However, a hybrid work environment can and often does include changes in social interaction and the use of collaboration technologies. In hybrid work, job crafting implicates potential changes in job and task contents, physical locations and workplaces and their quality; the composition of the needed digital tools; social relations in work and family; and temporal issues, that is, when, for how long and how often something happens; in addition to changes in one's mindset and behaviour, that is, attitudes and cognitive processes. In hybrid work, opportunities to craft workspace elements, sub-elements and their features vary. For example, in mobile multilocational work, it can be difficult to influence the quality of physical locations; working conditions on trains or at the customer's place are given, and it is easier to adapt to them than to change them. However, it is important to acknowledge that job crafting in hybrid work is related to home crafting and leisure crafting. While leisure crafting is about changing task and relational boundaries of leisure activities, home crafting is about changing home demands and resources. Verelst et al. (2023) studied how full-time teleworkers combine job and home crafting during the day, as this can optimise employees' well-being. Their findings show that daily job and home crafting were negatively related to daily energy depletion. However, too much daily job and home crafting does not work; combining high daily job and home crafting was related to higher energy depletion compared to moderate crafting levels.

Wessels et al. (2019) suggest that when place and time use change, employees need to engage in 'time-spatial crafting'. This implies that employees in knowledge work organisations optimise time and spatial demands daily, and engage dynamically in time-spatial job crafting. This should help them to capitalise on flexibility on a day-to-day basis. Wessels et al. (2019) suggest that in each context, employees need to reflect on different options to craft, make actual choices to act, and then act, addressing changing conditions. Job crafting is a continuous process. Individuals cope with changing demands by crafting their resources; for example, by developing their abilities and skills to consciously choose the best place for a certain task and set up workspaces wherever or whenever is best.

EXPERIENCES WITH HW IMPLEMENTATION DURING THE PANDEMIC

Next, early experiences with implementing hybrid work in organisations based in Europe are reported (Vartiainen and Vanharanta, 2023). The focal question was: How have companies implemented hybrid work or how are they planning to do so?

The data were collected at the end of the second year of the pandemic, 2021, when many companies and other organisations started to design, implement and test hybrid work arrangements. Most companies did not yet have much experience with hybrid work systems at the time of data collection, but were planning hybrid work arrangements based on their experiences with company-wide remote work during the pandemic. First, the data analysis process is described. Following this, the findings sub-section focuses on the ways HW has been organised or is planned to be organised in companies and other organisations in Europe; what kinds of support structures, policies and spatial arrangements are considered important for the success of HW; and what kinds of managerial challenges have been identified in these organisations that should be considered when implementing hybrid work.

Data and Analysis

The country reports (N = 27) from each country, and other online documents that were linked to the country reports, contained examples of the implementation of hybrid work from 80 organisations. These organisations represented 21 sectors, including finance (N = 23), IT and telecommunications (N = 19), insurance (N = 6), public administration (N = 6), utilities (N = 6), online retail (N = 3), and others (N = 17). Examples of how hybrid work has been implemented included information on the motivation for implementing HW, support structures and practices that facilitate HW, agreements and policies related to HW, how office space has been adapted to HW, and managerial challenges related to HW. The examples were analysed with a data-driven approach, focusing on the aspects of hybrid work that were brought up in the case descriptions. The aspects were coded based on the topic they were describing; for example, when the document contained explanations related to the reasons why hybrid work was implemented, this was coded as 'motivation for implementation: xx', where xx refers to the given reason in each case. For example, 'motivation for implementation: to attract new employees'. Finally, all quotations related to the motivation for implementing HW were organised into sub-groups based on the specific driver. This approach resulted in five general themes:

- Agreements and policies related to HW (N = 108).
- Support structures and practices that facilitate HW (N = 53).
- Managerial challenges related to HW (N = 30).
- Motivation for implementing HW (N = 27).
- How office space has been adapted to HW (N = 22).

Quotations related to these themes were organised into 5–12 sub-categories. In addition, countries and industries were coded for each quotation.

Findings: Implementing Hybrid Work

Based on the above analysis of the country reports, this sub-section describes how European organisations have implemented or are planning to implement HW. The examples include information on agreements and policies related to HW, support structures and practices that facilitate HW, managerial challenges related to HW, information on the motivation for implementing HW, and how office space has been adapted to HW. The frequency of each of these themes and their sub-categories are summarised in Table 7.2.

Table 7.2 Critical factors in implementing HW: summary of themes and sub-categories

THEME	CONTENT
Agreements and policies (N = 107)	• Specific number of days/weeks at the office required (N = 40) • General policies related to space and location (N = 22) • Employees' freedom to choose the location (N = 15) • Policy regarding working hours (N = 7) • Specific percentage of monthly work time spent at the office or remotely defined (N = 7) • Specific number of days per year allowed for working abroad (N = 6) • Local, team-level agreement (N = 5) • Conditions for HW (N = 5) • Costs (N = 3)
Support structures and practices (N = 53)	• Technology and applications (N = 13) • Training and guidelines (N = 13) • Communication and virtual events (N = 12) • Grant for furnishing home office (N = 9) • Support for mental and physical well-being (N = 6)
Managerial challenges (N = 30)	• Communication and information sharing (N = 6) • Interpersonal relationships and sense of community (N = 5) • Ensuring well-being (N = 4) • Adaptive management approach (N = 4) • Addressing employee needs (N = 4) • Creating a culture of trust (N = 4) • Other (N = 3)

THEME	CONTENT
Motivation for implementation HW (N = 27)	• To increase employee productivity, motivation, and well-being (N = 8) • To maintain organisational culture and cohesion (N = 4) • To attract new employees (N = 3) • To provide structure and stability for employees (N = 2) • To maintain flexibility and autonomy (N = 2) • To reduce office space costs (N = 2) • To eliminate commute (N = 2)
Office space adaptation (N = 22)	• No assigned desks (N = 5) • Multifunctional office (N = 5) • More meeting rooms (N = 3) • Less office space (N = 3) • Community space (N = 3) • Other (N = 5)

Source: Vartiainen and Vanharanta (2023, pp. 55–56).

Agreements and Policies

The agreements and policies discussed in the reports were mainly related to *organisation-specific solutions* in terms of the required number of days in the office when adopting HW. Most organisations required employees to spend 1–3 days at the office per week, but there were various ways in which this was defined (Box 7.1). In some organisations, for example, a minimum number of telework days was defined; whereas in others, the policies defined the minimum number of days spent at the office. This did not apply to all personnel, however, as not all jobs are compatible with remote working. In many organisations, employees were grouped into those who were permanently at the office, those who were permanent remote workers, and those who could adopt a hybrid model. In several examples, employees who could work remotely had complete freedom to choose where they worked; in others, their work needed to be conducted within the country, but otherwise it was flexible. In some organisations, a specific number of working days that an employee could work abroad was defined. In some cases, teams were given autonomy and responsibility to agree, based on team-specific needs, on the number and organisation of office work days. Additionally, general policies regarding the use of office space were presented. For example, one German company, which reduced the number of work stations, and did not offer fixed stations, agreed that if no working spaces were available, the employee would be free to leave after one hour and end their working day.

BOX 7.1 AGREEING ON SCHEDULING

The model of hybrid work implemented in the Municipality permits workers whose functions allow them to telework a maximum of four days per week, requiring, in all situations, that at least one of the weekly working days must be in-person and that on one of the days of the week, the team must work together in-person. (PT, public administration)

Support Structures and Practices

Organisations implementing HW identified supporting practices and structures that were considered to facilitate its success. Technological tools and applications were the most central category of support structures. Technologies, such as different virtual platforms that facilitate online collaboration, were considered valuable types of communication tools when meeting face-to-face is not possible (Box 7.2). In addition, companies have developed novel systems; for example, for monitoring the availability of and reserving work stations at the office. Management and employee training and guidelines were mentioned in several cases as important support structures. For example, training for managing remote teams, health and safety guides for working from home, and employee training in digital skills and data security, have been provided. Regular formal and informal communication practices, and virtual events to ensure a sense of community and organisational culture, have been put in place. In several organisations, an allowance was provided for furnishing an ergonomic home office. Finally, novel support structures for maintaining physical and mental well-being in HW were put in place. For example, in a Cypriot consultancy, a psychologist is available 24/7 for employees.

BOX 7.2 USING COLLABORATION TECHNOLOGIES

When previously most of the communication and activities were face-to-face, then now they have started using different virtual platforms like Slack, Confluence and Google products to facilitate communication. (EE, finance)

Managerial Challenges

The company cases included some specific HW-related managerial challenges that companies had identified, and issues which managers should address when managing and leading employees working in hybrid mode. These challenges require new competencies and training for managers. Based on their experiences, the companies found that they should pay specific attention to communication and information sharing, and facilitate the development and maintenance of interpersonal relationships (Box 7.3). Relatedly, a culture of trust was considered a prerequisite for the HW model to work. Additionally, the companies believed that the managerial approach should be flexible, that employee experiences should be constantly monitored, and that the organisation and its HW practices and policies should be adjusted according to employee- and team-level needs. A leader can share power, put the needs of the employees first, and help people to develop and perform as well as possible. Another challenge for managers is ensuring employee well-being when managers do not have the ability to ascertain their subordinates' situation at any time.

BOX 7.3 DEVELOPING MANAGEMENT AND LEADERSHIP PRACTICES

For the workplace of the future to contribute to a strong employee experience, managers and leadership need to create the conditions for and encourage strong collegial interaction in both the physical and digital environment. Maintaining and strengthening collegial interaction when we are not always physically on-site becomes even more important. This requires a strategic focus on maintaining and strengthening interaction, both by staff and managers. (SE, research)

Motivation for Implementation of HW

The motivation to implement hybrid work was based, on one hand, on the positive experiences gained from remote work during the pandemic; and on the other hand, on the negative implications of not meeting in real time. This strengthened the view of hybrid work as a mixture of working at the office and remotely. The positive experiences were found to increase employee motivation, productivity and well-being. It was also considered a crucial factor in attracting new employees. The opportunities to reduce office space costs and eliminate commutes were mentioned as motivating factors for introducing HW and thereby maintaining the opportunity to work remotely. Additionally, organisations justified their motivation to implement HW as a way to maintain organisational culture and group cohesion, as well as to provide structure and stability to employees by encouraging them to spend time at the office. Face-to-face meetings were also considered important from the perspective of knowledge sharing and organisational innovativeness. Thus, HW was justified as an opportunity not only to maintain autonomy and flexibility (Box 7.4), but also to maintain social relationships and provide structure and stability for employees.

BOX 7.4 INCREASING FLEXIBILITY

In the past, you had to take a day off when the chimney sweeper came. Now I'm logging out for ten minutes. This leads to more satisfaction and productivity. (AT, energy)

Rather rarely, excerpts underlined environmental sustainability issues as benefits and opportunities of implementing telework. They emphasised time savings due to less commuting and avoiding traffic jams and thus reduced carbon dioxide (CO_2) emissions. For example, Greenpeace Germany commissioned a study published in August 2020 which concluded that 5.4 million tonnes of carbon emissions could be saved if 40 per cent of the employees worked from home regularly two days per week. This would amount to reducing the emissions caused by commuter traffic by 18 per cent.

How Office Space has been Adapted to HW

In some company cases, the changes to office space already made or considered necessary to better support HW were described. Many examples highlighted the need for more meeting rooms as opposed to single work stations, as the office would be used primarily for meetings and spending time with colleagues. Some organisations have been transforming their spaces into multifunctional offices to better cater to individual- and team-specific work needs, and to make the space more efficient and attractive (Box 7.5). The need for attractive community spaces was highlighted. Additionally, some organisations reported moving to smaller spaces, as most of the workforce would be working remotely for a significant portion of the week, and thus individually assigned desks were not needed. The office space, in many cases, was described as a community space and a place for meeting colleagues rather than concentrating within a traditional office setting. Accordingly, the office designs featured group work elements and more meeting rooms than in a traditional office. Some organisations reported establishing working hubs in more remote areas, for those employees who live further away from the main office but wish to work outside their homes. As an interesting example of municipality-level support for HW, the city of Vilnius has set up mobile work stations in the city centre equipped with Wi-Fi for anyone to use free of charge.

BOX 7.5 CASE EXAMPLE: IMPLEMENTATION OF HW

A Hungarian financial institution with 3300 employees made the decision to switch permanently to a hybrid working model once the pandemic situation allows a return to the office. This means that in jobs where remote work is possible, employees must spend at least half of their monthly working hours in the office. Working hours are flexible. Employees are free to allocate their working time between 7 a.m. and 8 p.m. Meetings can only be organised between 8 a.m. and 5 p.m.

The decision to implement HW was driven by the employees' general need for flexibility and the increasing labour shortage in the banking sector. Moreover, based on an internal survey, 90 per cent of the employees considered working from home to be as effective as working at the office. With this arrangement, the company seeks to maintain trust and loyalty among existing employees and to attract talented young employees.

In the hybrid work arrangement, the primary function of the office building is to serve as a community space and a place for maintaining personal relationships and team cohesion. The office has been prepared for hybrid work by updating the meeting rooms with video and audio technologies to support the involvement of remote workers in meetings.

CORE ISSUES IN THE IMPLEMENTATION OF HW

Identifying the Benefits

The motivation to implement HW is driven, on the one hand, by the positive implications of telework, such as the employer's opportunity to apply flexible working structures, and the employee's increased autonomy and decreased need to commute, which have been positively associated with employee productivity, motivation and well-being. In addition, employers value the implementation of HW as a motivator and an opportunity to attract new employees and reduce office space costs. These are indeed familiar implications related to traditional remote and telework, and are thus expected to apply to HW as well. On the other hand, the implementation of HW is also justified by highlighting the opportunity to provide structure and stability for employees, and to maintain organisational culture and cohesion by also ensuring face-to-face interaction at the organisation's premises.

Autonomy-enhancing Culture

For many organisations, the shift to HW provides an opportunity to change the organisational culture towards agility by providing employees more influence in deciding on the time and place of their work, based on their tasks and personal preferences. The right to determine schedules, make task-related decisions, and select work methods, increases individual agility resources. An agile organisational culture also requires trust between actors, which helps to build a culture of trust in organisations if HW is implemented in a way that sustains individual- and team-level productivity and well-being. Agility also entails the flexibility of management: monitoring the employee and team-level experience, and adjusting the organisation, practices and policies of HW according to changing needs.

Agreements

While in the telework literature the focus has been primarily on the individual and, for example, task independence has been highlighted as one of the success factors of telework, the HW discussion considered a team-level agreement to be a viable approach for ensuring functional HW organisation. The increase in the number of remote workers means changes in team-level operations, which should be agreed upon among the team members. Moreover, team-level needs are also central when developing the physical environment in the office for face-to-face meetings. In many companies, the office space has been adapted to facilitate teamwork and maintain a sense of community by providing more spaces for serendipitous interaction.

Support Structure and Practices

The need for support structures and practices that ensure productivity and well-being, as well as maintain organisational culture and a sense of community, are other central issues considered when planning the organisation of HW. Support structures and practices include technologies, such as virtual platforms, that facilitate online collaboration when meeting face-to-face is not possible. Management and employee training and guidelines are needed, such as training for managing remote teams, and employee training in digital skills and data security, in addition to health and safety guides for working from home. Maintaining the organisational culture and a sense of community is addressed by establishing regular formal and informal face-to-face communication practices and virtual events. Several organisations have granted support for equipping an ergonomic work station in the home office; and new support structures, such as guided physical exercises and psychological support for those suffering from stress, have been introduced to maintain physical and mental well-being among HW employees.

Physical Premises

Moreover, both individual and team-level needs are central to developing the physical environment. If an employee is working at and from home, a proper ergonomic working environment is needed. Mobile and multilocational workplaces are more difficult to design, as an employee is dependent on local offerings. In many organisations, the office space is adapted to facilitate teamwork and maintain a sense of community by providing more spaces for serendipitous interaction than before. Overall, the meaning of the office seems to be shifting, from the primary place of work to a community space in which the main purpose is to meet and work with colleagues.

Mixtures of Physical, Virtual, Social and Temporal Elements

There are multiple options for implementing the physical, virtual, social and temporal elements of hybrid work. The feasibility of different arrangements depends on legislation, organisational and team-level objectives and agreements, task descriptions, and individual needs and preferences. Much of the HW discussion has revolved around what elements constitute hybrid work. The most common solution for the physical space has been to suggest a mixture of office and home. The temporal element has been more complicated to decide, as there are many options to consider: how often, when, and for how long, are hybrid working hours? The answer is most often the optimal number of telework days per week, and what kind of organisation-wide policies are needed to ensure that the benefits of both telework and in-office work are achieved. Most organisations require employees to spend 1–3 days at the office per week, but there are various ways to time the days; for example, perhaps Mondays and Fridays are office days. In some organisations, a maximum number of telework days is defined; for example, ten telework days per month. In others, the number of days, their timing and frequency are left to the team to decide, based on its needs. Social space arrangements have concerned social relations among employees with colleagues, superiors and the family at home. Virtual space solutions have focused on tools that enable communication, and collaboration tools to be functional and secure.

In the next chapter, hybrid work is considered from the viewpoint of leadership.

NOTE

1. A multi-space office comprises of different types of working areas which employees can choose from, depending on their task at hand. These include, for example, different types of collaboration spaces, open office spaces, and quiet areas for tasks that require concentration (e.g., Boutellier et al., 2008).

8. Management and leadership

Two important organisational-level issues arise in the transformation towards hybrid work: *how to manage work and lead people* in this change and after it. The transformation proceeds phase by phase, impacting upon the roles of management. In hybrid work, leaders on different levels – that is, senior management, middle managers and supervisors – become remote workers, and employees take on the role of self-leadership. The management perspective becomes concrete in hybrid work when decisions are made on the organisational level concerning the realisation of the goals of an organisation, and especially the arrangements of physical and virtual spaces, social relations and time use. Management's role and responsibility in the design, implementation and use of hybrid work are to care for internal and external relations and resources, and frame and organise the transformation and actual working in the new context. The role of leadership is central to get employees involved in concrete implementation and adaptation processes, and to develop working practices further.

MANAGEMENT GOALS AND EXPECTATIONS

Management is how businesses organise and direct workflow, operations and employees to meet organisational goals. Management can decide *between a top-down or bottom-up approach*, or choose their combination, when designing and implementing hybrid work. Top-down would mean weighting the organisation's goals, resources and competencies, and bottom-up would mean paying attention to employees' needs. Many of the organisational – and at the same time, management's – expectations of using flexible forms of work have been discussed in Chapter 2, which concerned the flexibility paradigm. The *management perspective* considers flexible working as a productivity or efficiency resource, and a strategic issue for organisations. The *people perspective* primarily emphasises individual agency and the well-being of employees in the context of organisational culture and structure. Illegems and Verbeke (2004), in their resource-based model, sorted the ambivalent impacts of telework adoption into five dilemmatic categories that might influence management decisions. First, the strategic development of human capital, for example, enhanced recruiting potential versus reduced employee loyalty. Second, the operational functioning of the human capital, for example, increased work time versus reduced promotion potential. Third, the organisation's broader productive efficiency; for example, improved flexibility versus investments in information and communication technology (ICT). Fourth, the organisation's external linkages; for example, the image of the organisation. And fifth, externalities, for example job opportunities for disabled persons versus ambiguities in labour legislation. In the best case scenario, an organisation's resources will grow.

Expectations During the Pandemic

The employers' and management's expectations regarding the goals of transitioning to hybrid work were investigated in the European Questionnaire Study (Vartiainen and Vanharanta, 2023, pp. 35–40) during the COVID-19 pandemic. At the *organisational level*, targets were cost savings, mainly due to reduced office space needs, new opportunities to recruit new workers, new practices, and increased productivity. From the perspective of an organisation, hybrid work was expected to provide an opportunity (but also a requirement) to reconsider and redesign types of work contracts, digitalise work processes and procedures by diversifying ICT use, develop office spaces to meet the needs of hybrid employees better, and develop human resources (HR) and managerial practices and guidelines. The need for new competencies requires training, and collaboration requires fluent communication.

Companies focused on the concrete issues of telework from home and hybrid work. Many of them expected new forms of work to continue when the pandemic ends. Benefits and possible positive impacts were expected in terms of work efficiency, better adjustment of work obligations and private life, a reduction in stress felt by employees, and reduced business costs. One of the issues discussed was the reduced need for office space due to options such as desk sharing. A reduction in the office space needed by a company was expected to substantially reduce costs. Some companies also had a clear tendency to occupy office buildings in more central areas than before, to be close to employee housing, as this arrangement would save them time in commuting. Companies often use such opportunities to inform the public about their flexible working arrangements, to attract young employees. Concerns were related to the availability and quality of equipment for workers to use at home (laptops, mobile phones) and the work–life balance of employees.

Employer unions' representatives generally suggested that telework should be regulated among social partners within the process of the definition or the renewal of collective agreements, and not through legal means. For them, the European Framework on Telework (ETUC et al., 2002) was found to work well, and no additional legislation was needed, only good examples and best practices. It was stated that many companies have already made good progress with their employees by applying internal company regulations to hybrid work. Employers' concerns focused on unilateral decisions by public authorities regarding the compulsory character of telework during the pandemic crisis. Other concerns were also reported; for example, the right to reversibility, benefits, and the right to privacy were regarded as already sufficiently detailed in existing legislation.

A survey conducted by McKinsey (Alexander et al., 2021) confirms that most organisations also see value in hybrid work and were planning to combine remote and on-site working after the pandemic. Most executives expected that employees would be on site between 21 and 80 per cent of the time, or one to four days per week. While the shift to remote work during the pandemic had positive effects – for example, on productivity – in some organisations (Alexander et al., 2021), management observed differences in managing remotely versus in person, and experienced difficulties in leading their organisations. For example, in their interview study of 50 executives on their experiences with leading their organisations during the pandemic, Kane et al. (2021) uncovered several challenges. In managing remote workers, innovation capability weakened because serendipitous connections in collaboration with others dropped off precipitously. In addition, there were challenges in starting new projects relying on virtual collaboration; and establishing and maintaining organisational culture was difficult, if not impossible, in a virtual setting. Employees, particularly younger employees, received less mentoring and coaching during the shift to remote work than they did before the pandemic.

Management Change

The transformation to hybrid work triggers a shift from direct supervision to management by objectives, and to a supportive leadership style that emphasises trust-based relationships, and remote workers' empowerment and self-control. Pianese et al. (2023) state that supervision and control in remote work are a primary concern for managers, and constitute a severe barrier to the adoption and diffusion of work arrangements. Management must be aware of their impacts. *Organisational control* is defined (ibid., p. 327) as a 'set of mechanisms aimed at aligning employees' capabilities, activities, and performances to organisational aspirations and objectives'. Pianese et al. synthesised studies on how physical distance implied in working remotely influences organisational control, according to five control domains. In addition to output control, control is enacted top-down by managers, for example through their leadership style and building trusting social relationships; and by organisations, for example by fostering organisational identification, as well as bottom-up by building remote and teleworkers' work identities. Pianese et al. also identified various control mechanisms of remote workers: behaviour control, exercised through the definition of rules and procedures regulating task execution; output control, focused on measurable objectives assigned to employees; peer control, exerted by colleagues; self-control of employees; and clan control, based on shared norms, beliefs and values within a group or an organisation. These control systems are established by organisations setting objectives but mediated by managers. Managers emphasising trust-based relationships with employees balance emotional-focused with job-focused support. Remote workers reinforce norms of control appreciating clear objectives and autonomy. The technological and social support promote this process.

One of the issues discussed during the pandemic was *surveillance*, its ethicality, and its impacts. Aloisi and De Stefano (2022, p. 298) refer to data showing that in April 2020 demand for tracking tools surged by 54 per cent, and was on average 58 per cent higher in 2021 than it was before the pandemic. Tracking can be done in many ways. For example, someone's location is tracked via Global Positioning System (GPS). The productivity of manufacturing employees is followed by asking them to wear radio-frequency identification (RFID) technologies. Interactions are captured via body cameras. During the pandemic, there was discussion about the functionality and ethicality of electronic performance monitoring (EPM), or the use of technological means to observe, record and analyse information that directly or indirectly relates to employee job performance. In their meta-analysis, Ravid et al. (2023) did not find evidence that EPM improves worker performance; instead, it increases worker stress. Their findings also demonstrate that organisations which monitor more transparently and less invasively can expect more positive attitudes from workers. They concluded that best practices in human resource management, such as honesty, procedural transparency and providing individuals with control over their own work, continue to be important mechanisms for guiding workers towards individual and organisational goals.

Managing in Hybrid Contexts

An issue is how to manage work in a hybrid context. In an early telework management study, Pearlson and Saunders (2001) identified three paradoxes from the management's perspective. First, increased flexibility and increased structure. Flexibility allows freedom for employees to choose a place and time when the work is done. However, new structures are needed to provide spaces that support working and, for example, to schedule official meetings. Second, greater individuality, and more teamwork. On the individual level, tasks well suited to teleworking are those that can be performed in isolation. However, teamwork is the most common way today to work and collaborate for a common goal. Third, more responsibility and greater control. Though employees can do their tasks independently, managers want to understand and evaluate employees doing their jobs and their output. The question of control is critical; and its nature is ambivalent.

One of the management's interests is to avoid *counterproductive* workplace behaviours, and to know the factors that influence them in remote work. Traditionally, counterproductivity is seen in voluntary acts intended to harm the organisation or its employees, involving theft, lateness, interpersonal abuse, sabotage, and so on. Cyberloafing or cyberslacking has been said to be a potential form of counterproductivity in teleworking organisations. *'Cyberloafing'* is defined as employees' voluntary use of organisations' Internet resources for non-work-related activities during official working hours, or as 'personal Internet use at work' (Lim and Teo, 2022, p. 3). Managers may view cyberloafing as a workplace behaviour that must be regulated, whereas employees can perceive it as rest and recovery from excessive demands. Lim and Teo argue in their wide review that cyberloafing has a dualistic nature, in that it can be counterproductive or restorative. Because of dissatisfaction with the organisation, a lack of interest in or boredom with the tasks at hand, cyberloafing can lead, for example, to lower work productivity. A moderate amount of cyberloafing can be healthy, allowing employees to recharge before transitioning back to work; and re-energising fuels employees' creativity, enabling them to approach work more effectively.

LEADERSHIP ROLES AND EXPERIENCES IN TRANSFORMATION

Hybrid Leadership

In general, leadership is influencing people to achieve the organisation's goals. In shared leadership, mutual influence towards a common goal is key (Han and Hazard, 2022). *Hybrid leadership* occurs both in person and digitally. However, hybrid leadership is more than just leading with the help of technologies and on site. The roles and tasks of individual leaders vary because of varying contextual demands and employee needs. Each hybrid work configuration is different, depending on the physical locations of superiors and employees, the share of face-to-face and online interaction, the availability of digital tools, the climate of social interaction, including the psychological contract, and the personal resources of hybrid workers. The psychological contract refers to mutual beliefs, perceptions and informal unwritten obligations between an employer and an employee (Rousseau, 1989). This contract is under pressure when working from anywhere is changed from a privilege for a few, to an option for all employees who feel entitled to it. In addition, the demands of leadership change over time, impacting upon roles in different phases of the transformation. Superiors' tasks as leaders are to help employees eliminate potential hindrances, and develop challenges in their work and other life into opportunities and resources in the design, implementation and use of hybrid work. Superiors have a strong negotiation power over who has access to hybrid work, and how employees are supported in hybrid working.

What kinds of tasks and roles would superiors have in hybrid work? The *task-oriented leadership style* focuses more on what systems can lead to greater self-efficacy. *Relationship-oriented leadership* focuses on team members' well-being and growth. According to the *functional leadership theory* (Morgeson et al., 2010), the role of the leader is to satisfy the needs of followers to improve their work outcomes. They developed a taxonomy of 15 critical team leadership functions and grouped them into the transition and action phases. These phases are understood here as the implementation and use phases of the hybrid work on both individual and group levels. The transition (implementation) phase is a period when an individual or a team focus on activities related to planning and organising work and evaluating the performance such that an employee or a team will ultimately be able to achieve its goal or objective. The action (use) phase is when a hybrid worker or team is focused on activities that directly contribute to accomplishing its goals. The 15 leadership functions (Morgeson et al., 2010, p. 10) in the transition phase include composing, defining a mission, establishing expectations and goals, structuring and planning, training and developing, sensemaking, and providing feedback. In the action phase, the functions are monitoring, managing boundaries, challenging, performing tasks, solving problems, providing resources, encouraging self-management, and supporting social climate.

These leadership functions are realised both face-to-face and digitally. Digital technologies are expected to play a critical role in the communication and collaboration of hybrid work, as shown during the pandemic. Digital leadership or e-leadership is defined (Avolio et al., 2000, p. 617) as: 'a social influence process mediated by AIT (= Advanced Information Technology) to produce a change in attitudes, feelings, thinking, behaviour, and/or performance with individuals, groups, and/or organizations'. From the leadership function list, Bell et al. (2023) suggest four leadership functions to have stronger effects in virtual as compared to face-to-face environments: (1) encouraging self-management; (2) defining mission; (3) establishing expectations and goals; and (4) supporting the social climate. In addition, they add to the function list 'facilitating the use of technology'.

Leadership Experiences in Virtual Teams and Remote and Telework

Leadership in virtual teams

In hybrid work, leadership concerns the change, tasks, and leader–employee and leader–team relationships. Many former studies on remote leadership are about leading virtual teams (VTs). As Costa et al. (2021, p. 619) note, VTs are now a ubiquitous feature of organisations, bringing challenges for vital team processes, including coordination, information exchange and interpersonal relationships, as well as for many other fundamental aspects, such as the leadership of emotional exchanges. In rich research spanning over three decades, researchers have shown that technology-mediated leadership is an important contributor to the success and performance of virtual teams (e.g., Gilson et al., 2015; Höddinghaus et al., 2023).

Reviews on virtual teams have revealed the need for strong leadership, where a formal leader is essential when building trust, commitment and team identity, and in leading and tracking team progress (Gibbs et al., 2017). The style and context of leadership may have an impact. In a recent meta-analysis, Brown et al. (2021) applied the functional leadership theory and found that both relationship-focused and task-focused leadership positively relate to virtual team performance. Team size and task interdependence also impact upon performance: relationship-focused leadership is a stronger predictor of performance for larger teams, whereas task-focused leadership is a weaker predictor of team performance in virtual teams with high task interdependence. Höddinghaus et al. (2023), in their systematic overview, also found predominantly positive correlations between task-oriented, relational-oriented and *change-oriented leadership*, and follower reactions – that is, job performance and attitudes – within highly virtual work contexts. Moreover, higher levels of virtuality increased the effects of task-oriented and some relational-oriented leadership styles; while mixed findings were found for change-oriented leadership. These findings suggest the relative amount of electronically mediated leader–follower interaction as the core element of leadership in virtual work settings. This underlines the role of e-leadership or digital leadership in hybrid work.

Leadership in remote and telework

In a past telework study, Golden and Veiga (2008) had found that the *extent of working in a virtual mode* impacts upon superior–subordinate relationships: those with high-quality relationships, who also extensively worked virtually, demonstrated the highest levels of commitment, job satisfaction and performance, in comparison to those who worked less extensively virtually. Those with lower-quality relationships who worked extensively in the virtual mode demonstrated lower commitment and job satisfaction, but performed somewhat better than those who worked a limited amount in this mode. In a later study, Golden and Fromen (2011) compared three managerial work modes (traditional, telework and virtual work) to investigate differences in employee work experiences and outcomes. Their results suggested that unlike employees with managers in the traditional work mode, work experiences and outcomes were generally less positive for employees with teleworking managers who spend a portion of the week away from the office, and they are lower as well for employees with virtual managers who are away from the office full-time. Being a teleworking leader is challenging.

In addition to the challenges of leading remotely in 'forced' working from home (WFH), teleworking leaders also have common challenges with their teleworking employees. For example, Golden and Fromen (2011) found that employees with teleworking managers responded less positively than employees of traditional managers when they considered their work experiences such as feedback and workload, and outcomes such as job satisfaction and turnover intentions. Hence, working at home seems to generate uncertainty and unpredictability concerning employees' and their leaders' relationships. Because of reduced interaction, there is a lack of social contact and isolation from the flow of information, support and help from management and colleagues. The unpredictability of some of the work causes a particular concern. For example, how would a leader know whether a worker had truly encountered a problem that took longer to resolve than expected, or whether the worker was slacking off? O'Neill et al. (2014) found that leaders also expressed protective concerns for their staff, as they worried that workers may be struggling with a work-related issue, or struggling in general with working from home. They were concerned that when working from home, workers may not always receive important information in a timely manner. Overall, it seems that working and leading remotely create additional challenges for leaders.

Leadership Experiences during the Pandemic

Studies on leadership during the pandemic show that teleworking was more intensive for leaders than their former face-to-face working style, impacting upon their employees' actions. A five-day diary study of 84 leaders (Venz and Boettcher, 2021) shows that perceived COVID-19-related work intensification was positively linked to leaders' work time spent dealing with emails as well as appraised email overload, leading to leaders' exhaustion. The frequency of interaction with leaders, and the beliefs of employees about a leader's role, affected teleworkers' effort, performance and withdrawal. Using a three-wave survey with 260 respondents working remotely, Carsten et al. (2021) found that teleworkers with a co-production role orientation, who see their role as more collaborative, reported higher levels of effort in work under conditions of high leader interaction. However, teleworkers with passive role orientations reported less effort when leader interaction was high, and the mediational chain predicting job performance and withdrawal was contingent on the frequency of leader interaction.

Moreover, it seems that *leaders changed their leadership style* in the first phase of the pandemic. For example, Stoker et al. (2021) show in their online survey study that managers executed significantly less direct control and delegated more to employees. Employees also perceived a significant decrease in control, but perceived, on average, no change in delegation. Employees of lower-level managers even reported a significant decrease in delegation. Overall, their results show that increased delegation is associated with employees' increased perceived productivity and higher ratings of leadership quality. These study examples on leadership during the early phase of the pandemic show that the swift change in working contexts matters, and the job demands of both employees and leaders working from home change, requiring changes in job and personal resources.

An Example Study: Janus-faced and Dual-role Leadership

Challenges and benefits in WFH, and their ambivalences, were studied (Vartiainen, 2023) by using the job demands–resources (JD-R) model (Bakker, 2011; Demerouti et al., 2001) as the framework. The study focused on challenge demands during the pandemic by asking what kinds of challenges teleworking from home poses for teleworking leaders. The study shows that telework from home is 'Janus-faced': telework is simultaneously challenging and rewarding in several respects. In addition, teleworking leaders have a dual role, as they must adapt to working at home as teleworkers themselves, and to being leaders of teleworkers.

Methodology

Survey data were collected immediately after the lockdown in spring 2020 (Blomqvist et al., 2020). The survey included two open-ended questions: 'What has been the most challenging in your work during the COVID-19 crisis? Think broadly about your individual work as well as your collaboration with your colleagues or balancing work–family issues', and 'What has been the most rewarding in your work during the COVID-19 (Corona) crisis? Think broadly about your individual work as well as your collaboration with your colleagues or balancing work–family issues.' From the responses to these questions, an independent sub-set of data was filtered concerning teleworking leaders in small and medium-sized enterprises (SMEs) with fewer than 50 paid employees.

In total, the leaders' responses (N = 195) included 368 quotations concerning challenges (N = 201) or rewards/benefits (N = 167) as potential opportunities and resources. The coding process started deductively by using the following categories from the literature: work–life interface (e.g., Felstead and Henseke, 2017), leadership (e.g., Thielsch et al., 2020) and communication (e.g., Wang et al., 2020). As not all quotations (N = 41) could be coded based on prior knowledge, they were coded under the main category, working conditions. Most respondents reported challenges and rewards/benefits with different themes in WFH. In only 18 answers, the written response included both a challenge and a reward/benefit related to the same issue. For example, a leader wrote, 'Not having random interactions with people, for example, over coffee. These often create crucial new ideas. However, so many unnecessary meetings. It is a blessing to be able to concentrate on the study backgrounds instead of the everyday office hassle.'

This is an ambivalent answer, as the leader misses informal interaction with their employees (that is, a challenge). At the same time, however, the number of unnecessary meetings with them has decreased (that is, a reward/benefit).

Results: teleworking leaders' ambivalences in WFH

Overall, teleworking leaders perceived more challenges than rewards/benefits (Table 8.1). It is also seen that some of the respondents find only challenges in remote working and others only rewards/benefits as resources.

Most of the quotations were related to the *work–life interface*. The greatest challenges were not having the opportunity to concentrate on work at home, lengthened work days, and combining work and life. Alternatively, the greatest rewards and benefits acting as time and social resources were the time saved in commuting, the ability to concentrate on work, and the ability to spend more time with family (if there was a family). This showed that the family situation, for example, whether a person is living alone or with their family, explains much about managing work–life balance.

Leadership itself seems to be a real challenge for several reasons. On the one hand, there were many quotations about a quick and slightly chaotic change. Remote leadership practices were still under construction, and the issue was how to reorganise everyone's work at a fast pace, and to determine what the daily practices are in supervising everyone's remote work. On the other hand, many quotations were about a fast adjustment to the new leadership role when working from home.

A significant challenge related to leadership lies in *communication* and information sharing: face-to-face ad hoc meetings were missing, and there were too many virtual meetings. However, it seems that the working climate when collaborating online was good, as some leaders underlined togetherness: everyone worked together and supported each other. Inadequate *working conditions*, including challenges in information and communication technologies and workplace ergonomics, further weakened communication, although taking ICT into full usage was seen as a benefit.

Individual ambivalences emerged in the categories of the work–life interface (N = 14), communication (N = 3), and leadership. While some individual

Table 8.1 Challenges and benefits of WFH in teleworking leaders' experiences

CHALLENGES (N = 201)	REWARDS/BENEFITS (N = 167)
Work–life interface (N = 168)	
Concentration: Lack of quietness at home, for example, because of family (N = 35)	Ability to concentrate to work (N = 28)
Time management: Lengthened work days (N = 20)	Time saved in commuting and the ability to spend more time with family etc. (N = 67)
Work–life balance: Challenges in combining work and life (N = 13)	Ability to better balance work- and non-work life (N = 5)
Leadership (N = 85)	
Fast change: Chaos and uncertainty (N = 21)	Fast adjustment to the situation (N = 24)
Communication with employees: Keeping communication with employees at a good enough level (N = 13)	
Leading remotely: Leading remotely in general (N = 9)	Success in remote leading in general (N = 5)
Reorganising work: Need to reorganise everyone's work at a fast pace (N = 8)	
Supervising employees: Challenges in supervising what everyone's doing remotely (N = 5)	
Communications (N = 74)	
Lack of meetings: Lack of social, face-to-face interaction (N = 23)	Togetherness: Everyone working together and supporting each other (N = 26)
Information sharing: Challenges in sharing information (N = 17)	
Lack of ad hoc meetings: Lack of spontaneous meetings (N = 5)	
Increased number of meetings: More meetings because of no time for transitions needed (N = 3)	
Working conditions (N = 41)	
ICTs: Problems with insufficient ICTs (N = 15)	Taking ICTs into full usage (N = 12)
Ergonomics: Problems with insufficient working facilities (N = 14)	

Source: Vartiainen (2023, p. 280).

respondents were happy to spend more time with their family when everyone stayed at home, they also felt that it was a challenge for their work, since they were not able to concentrate on their work tasks. The responses of teleworking leaders clearly show their dual role: leaders found similar challenges and benefits concerning the work–life interface at home as teleworkers. However, remote work also seems to increase leadership-related challenges in their work. The main demand characteristics of teleworking leaders were related to task-related communication, the ability to concentrate on work at home, and functional working conditions. 'Strong' leadership (Gibbs et al., 2017) is more demanding due to the experience of the change as chaotic and fast, as well as due to challenges in communication and supervising employees' actions remotely, while 'best processes' and 'best practices' are missing. Communication challenges appeared as missing social, face-to-face and ad-hoc meetings, as well as the increased number of online meetings. Without face-to-face meetings, communication and knowledge sharing were considered difficult. It was challenging to maintain high-quality relationships with employees, which can lower their commitment, job satisfaction and performance, as shown by Golden and Veiga (2008). Challenges in organising work in the home context were seen as work intensification (Venz and Boettcher, 2021). This included difficulty concentrating in a noisy home environment, feelings of chaos, lengthening work days, and balancing work and other life. There were also problems with insufficient ICTs and working facilities. This can lead to leaders' exhaustion in the long run.

Development of Hybrid Leadership

Quite a variety of leadership competencies and practices are needed in designing, implementing and using hybrid work. Hybrid leadership is not only about leaders and followers and how they interact, but also about seeing that other aspects in our environment lead us. As theorised earlier in this book, different configurations of hybrid work elements, sub-elements, and their features form the dynamic platform of hybrid leadership.

Past experiences of management and leadership from flexible work such as remote and telework and virtual teams, in addition to the findings concerning obligatory telework during the pandemic, show that from the leaders' viewpoint hybrid work will also be *'Janus-faced'*, that is, create ambivalent perceptions among those doing it. In addition, leaders will have *a dual role* as flexible managers of flexible workers. Flexible working is simultaneously challenging, but also empowering. For example, working in isolation from co-workers, for example, working at home, in isolation from co-workers, and in mostly basic working conditions, also provides some autonomy to leaders. The dual leader role is shown in superiors being themselves tele- or hybrid workers, managing and leading similar kinds of full-time and part-time employees, and freelancers. In this evolving 'new normal', leaders must adapt to new contexts and their dual role by learning new leadership competencies and encouraging their employees to lead themselves.

Socially, mediated communication can weaken social ties between co-workers and management, cause loneliness and also, on the other hand, cause tiredness due to constant online meetings and a deluge of emails. These are just a few of the challenges to meet when adapting to flexible ways of working. Moreover, in contemporary workplaces, it is not simply a question of face-to-face or virtual communication, but of both: organisational members may work with both types of media simultaneously, and at least often interweave their use. In their diary study, Bakker et al. (2021) showed how employees, by using proactive work strategies – that is, daily self-leadership and crafting their own jobs – could satisfy their basic psychological needs and facilitate job performance. They suggested that leaders could provide autonomy and feedback to employees to foster this kind of proactivity.

Teleworkers during the pandemic did not consider the remoteness of their leaders as a challenge, though their own autonomy and self-leadership were seen as both a challenge and a benefit. This clearly reflects the potential and need to develop employees' self-leadership skills as personal resources. As shown in many recent and past meta-analyses (e.g., Gajendran and Harrison, 2007), perceived autonomy enabling self-leadership is the most influential and extensive conveyor of telework effects. Teleworking leaders during the pandemic mostly raised challenges related to their own leadership in WFH, as can be expected (Golden and Fromen, 2011). The resources of WFH for them came from their job, that is, time savings, efforts building togetherness with colleagues, and ICT; in addition to social home resources, that is, support and energy received from their family.

Another common topic among teleworkers and teleworking leaders is how to arrange task- and relationship-related interactions in the changed social context, with different relations to colleagues and other actors (Brown et al., 2021). Both leaders and employees long for other people, which reflects feelings of loneliness in telework (Felstead et al., 2005).

The implication for leadership is that *leaders need to develop their personal resources and competencies*, which are both face-to-face and mediated communication and interaction skills, to help employees develop their technological, collaborative and self-leadership skills.

Based on the account above, the question arises regarding hybrid work: how can close daily face-to-face connections between a leader and an employee be replaced or balanced when employees and their leaders are all forced to work remotely from each other? Based on their observations on leadership practices in virtual teams, Kozlowski et al. (2021) suggested that in team-building, technological fluency should be ensured, in addition to establishing ground rules and norms for how the virtual team should function. In addition, a shared knowledge base is needed to build trust and team cohesion. To accomplish work, they suggested structural support, such as setting clear goals and instituting shared leadership among team members. Leading for the long haul requires maintaining trust and team cohesion, socialising new members, and balancing remote work with life and face-to-face work.

All in all, senior management, middle managers and supervisors need change-, task- and relationship-focused competencies and practices when designing, implementing and using hybrid work. Leaders and managers must restructure the organisation to be less hierarchical; learn, lead and communicate from a distance; and create functional working conditions for employees working from anywhere. Employees need autonomy to take responsibility and develop self-leadership competencies (e.g., Contreras et al., 2020). It is possible to evaluate the managerial support to a hybrid worker, for example, by using a five-item scale of managerial support to the teleworker developed by Mourão et al. (2023). The scale includes items regarding well-being, feedback, goal (assignment and follow-up), support and guidance (Box 8.1).

BOX 8.1 CONCEPTS AND ITEMS FROM THE BRIEF SCALE OF MANAGERIAL SUPPORT TO THE TELEWORKER

Constructive feedbacks (i.e., feedback): I get constructive feedback from my manager about my performance in remote activities, pointing me to opportunities for improvement.

Compatible goal assignment (i.e., goal assignment): the remote work goals assigned to me by my manager are compatible with the workload of my unit.

Support and guidance for tasks (i.e., guidance): I receive support from my manager when I ask for guidance to perform tasks remotely.

Goal tracking (i.e., goal follow-up): my manager tracks the achievement of work goals.

Health and welfare of subordinates (i.e., well-being): my manager demonstrates concern for my health and well-being.

Source: Based on Mourão et al. (2023, p. 169).

There are several leadership practices for how leaders can support hybrid work. First, to design and implement hybrid work, a trustful relationship, dialogical ways of interacting, and contracts stating the new rules and practices of the game, are needed between employers and workers. This includes agreeing on the ratio of days at the office and elsewhere. Second, a common understanding of the goals of an organisation should be built, tasks should be delegated, and good practices shared to maintain productivity and engagement.

Third, as underlined by Lautsch et al. (2009), superiors should stay in close contact with hybrid workers and provide emotional and social support rather than close monitoring; they must communicate frequently and well. This also includes promoting in-person meetings and events. Fourth, it is also crucial for teleworkers and teleworking leaders to learn to benefit from collaboration technologies, as they are important enablers of flexible working. In digital leadership, a competent e-leader needs to master how to choose, for single or combined use, the media that best suits their purposes and aims. Leaders should be effective in taking advantage of technology that enables virtual work, both synchronously and asynchronously. Fifth, leaders should encourage telecommuting employees to create work and life boundaries to reduce work–family ambivalence and manage it. Sixth, because of potential isolation, feelings of loneliness and mental health problems, leaders should progress the community spirit among employees. Seventh, to maintain and restore physical health and mental well-being as basic conditions for human activity, practices that revitalise personal resources must be developed. Eighth, managers should promote hybrid employees' self-leadership by encouraging and enabling self-directed work design, that is, job crafting.

9. Future hybrid work

It is not possible to step into the same river twice
(Heraclitus, *Herákleitos*; fl. c. 500 BC)

This final chapter concerns the future of hybrid work. Surveys worldwide show that the trend of flexible hybrid work arrangements is expected to continue. A global survey (Aksoy et al., 2023) shows that full-time employees worked from home 0.9 days per week, on average, looking across 34 countries in April–May 2023. Work from home (WFH) levels were higher in English-speaking countries. Full-time employees worked an average of 1.4 full-paid days per week from home across Australia, Canada, New Zealand, the United Kingdom, and the United States (US). By comparison, WFH levels average only 0.7 days per week in the seven Asian countries, 0.8 in the European countries, and 0.9 for four Latin American countries and South Africa. In the US, in October 2023: 57 per cent of employees worked full-time on site, 13 per cent were fully remote, and 30 per cent in a hybrid arrangement (Barrero et al., 2021). In a study[1] (Work 3.0), 42 per cent of leaders across the Asia Pacific expected that their company's employees post-COVID-19 would spend less than 50 per cent of their time on site at the company office. Similar findings are available from other continents. And, home and office are only single options of future locations to work in.

Today, the transformation of hybrid work continues, and it is a moving target. However, some normalisation and good practices are also occurring. Researcher and professional discussions since the pandemic have produced hybrid work scenarios to consider when practical solutions are in hand. In some of them, employees return to their main workplace, often blending remote work flexibility with on-site work, and typically working remotely two days a week. Many large companies and state and municipal organisations have formulated organisation-wide policies, giving some framework to tailored and localised work arrangements on the team and individual levels. Micro-, small and medium-sized companies have flexibly adapted to the new reality and organised activities.

HYBRID WORK IS HERE TO STAY

Needs for Continuous Change and Flexibility

The transition is not always smooth, and some upsets are expected, as are some unanswered questions. It is crucial to notice that hybrid work arrangements look different from the perspectives of individuals, their positions, teams and organisations. Returning to the main workplace has been justified by reasons related to organisational culture and the need for collaboration, innovations and creativity (Gibson et al., 2023). It has been argued that to develop, maintain and nurture their desired culture, organisations need to support in-person interactions; in-person interactions are needed to enable collaboration, relationships and connections, and spontaneous in-person encounters enhance innovativeness. However, these arguments, in their absolute sense, fail because culture, collaboration fluency and innovativeness depend not only on the location of working, but also on other elements of the working spaces. Hindrances, challenges, and benefits and opportunities differ as well as how to meet them. Questions emerge, such as: Who decides the place and timing of working? And are hybrid teams the same as virtual teams? Different factors impact upon their success. For example, for teams to succeed, shared understanding and collective mindsets, joint goals, relationships, mutual trust and team spirit play an important role. The form of hybrid work depends on its purpose and goals, context-related issues, available resources, and especially, what outcomes are expected regarding performance and well-being.

Many of the current open questions were presented above as individual-level hindrances and challenges, such as less access to work resources and equipment, feelings of isolation and loneliness, decreased collaboration and longing for colleagues, and ambivalent tensions such as the autonomy paradox when the workload is significantly increased and intensified due to expectations of constant availability and self-exploitation. On the other hand, employees look for greater autonomy in when, where and how they work, and even what they do. There are time savings based on reduced commuting. The balance between work and family and other life is a positive promise, but is also associated with the blurring of work and personal life. The feelings of autonomy can decrease with micro-managerial surveillance, following employees' performance and productivity, instead of trust-based shared and self-leadership. To overcome this autonomy–control paradox, Wheatley et al. (2023, p. 2) suggest 'a coordinated approach centred on "inclusive flexibility" and "responsible autonomy" that involves moving away from one-size-fits-all strategies towards a tailored approach offering employees choice, agency and voice in decision-making, while accommodating different stakeholder needs'.

An example of tensions on the team level is whether online interaction is a substitute for face-to-face interaction, or whether the two are complementary. In home working (HW), at least some of the collaboration occurs online using still-developing technologies. Another tension on the organisational level is that HW and fully remote work lead to lower office demand. This is a challenge to property owners: what should be done with extra office premises? One of the societal challenges is that remote-capable, teleworkable or hybridisable jobs constitute only part of the workforce, because of their responsibilities, and not all workplaces can flexibly organise their activities. Many frontline employees in service positions, such as nurses in health care and salespersons in shops, need close, face-to-face contact with their clients. Manufacturing products on the shop floor often requires the full-time presence or at least the keen attention of an employee. This difference may lead to the *'hybrid work divide'*, creating a group of privileged professions that enjoy autonomy and flexibility, while other groups are strictly tied to in-person work processes. However, from the perspective of HW as a combination of 'two or more things', these kinds of professions could also benefit from considering work content as a combination of basic work elements, sub-elements, and their features. It is possible to reformulate such jobs by rebuilding their structure to include previously missing elements and their features.

Technology as an Enabler

Technological development will be crucial as a material enabler of hybrid work, in addition to physical premises. Of the general global trends, the most immediate material factor affecting people's work activities and resources on the organisational level is the extensive utilisation of digitalisation, including the mobile Internet. In the Future of Jobs Survey by the World Economic Forum (Future of Jobs Report, 2023) covering 803 companies, more than 75 per cent of companies were looking to adopt big data, cloud computing and artificial intelligence (AI) in the next five years, transforming their organisation. Key applications in communications, working platforms and work process automation affect work and leisure and their relationship in many ways on the shop floor. Digital platforms and the transition to online and offline virtual work, the analysis and algorithmicising of extensive bulk data into intelligent cloud services, artificial intelligence, the 'Internet of Things' and the mobile Internet, machine learning, and robotisation are particularly associated with changes in the structure and contents of work; and possibly competencies. Automating work by replacing human work in production and distribution processes is not new. However, digitalisation of processes is shown in the development of sensors which translate the physical production process into digital information. This translation removes and replaces work phases by new, increasingly smart, hybrid digitalised phases and operations. The Internet of Things is one of the key technologies as it enables the connection of all the 'things' having an Internet Protocol (IP) address (such as smartphones, refrigerators, clothes and cars) to each other via the Internet. Information from those devices will then be a central part of the basic infrastructure and blend in with the physical reality.

Figure 9.1 shows the logic of the digitalisation penetration as a snowball effect: a technology affects a work process by transforming the micro-structure of its phases and operations, which is then mirrored in other components of the work system. The phases and operations of a value creation process are removed, hybridised or renewed, driven by decisions to implement and use digital smart technologies. As the value-producing process is usually still steered and managed by human activities, changes are also needed in division of human tasks and jobs. This, in turn, leads to a need to reorganise and structure organisations. Consequently, many other organisational and human-related issues are under pressure and need changes. For example, a restructuring and reorganising of work units is needed, resulting in new ways of working, leadership practices and competencies. The outcomes of this transformation are digitally influenced products and services, and changes in human mental space.

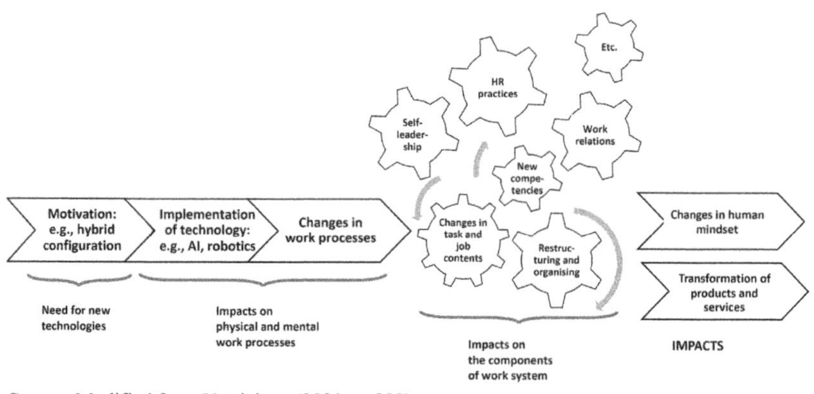

Source: Modified from Vartiainen (2020, p. 233).

Figure 9.1 The logic of digitalisation influence on work systems

It is evident that AI will strongly influence the contents and practices of hybrid work (Box 9.1), although how it exactly happens is still emerging. *Generative AI* refers to technologies that can identify patterns across large datasets and generate new content. By using machine learning algorithms, they generate content by pre-training on a large corpus of data, and then fine-tuning for specific tasks using human feedback. AI can not only converse and reason, but also remember the context of dialogues. This ability is generally expected of humans. The most advanced progress has happened in natural language capabilities, which are required for knowledge workers. While, for example, ChatGPT is focused on text, other AI systems from major platforms can generate images, video and audio. For example, the McKinsey Global Institute (Ellingrud et al., 2023) forecasts that automation affects a comprehensive set of work activities involving expertise, interaction with people, and creativity. Without generative AI, the institute estimates, automation could take over tasks accounting for 21.5 per cent of the hours worked in the US economy by 2030. With generative AI, that share can jump to 29.5 per cent.

BOX 9.1 AI EFFECTS ON PRODUCTIVITY AND QUALITY IN KNOWLEDGE WORK

Dell'Acqua et al. (2023) examined the performance implications of AI on complex and knowledge-intensive tasks of 758 consultants of Boston Consulting Group in Spring 2023. They were randomly assigned to one of three conditions. The first group (a control condition) proceeded without AI support; the second ('GPT Only') had the assistance of an AI tool based on GPT-4; and the third ('GPT + Overview') not only utilised the same AI tool but also benefited from supplementary prompt engineering overview, which increased the group's familiarity with AI.

The findings show that consultants using AI were significantly more productive, by completing 12.2 per cent more tasks on average, and 25.1 per cent more quickly, and produced significantly higher quality results, that is, more than 40 per cent higher quality compared to a control group. Consultants across the skills distribution benefited significantly from having AI augmentation, with those below the average performance threshold increasing by 43 per cent, and those above increasing by 17 per cent, compared to their own scores.

Further, the analysis shows the emergence of two distinctive patterns of successful AI use by humans along a spectrum of human–AI integration. One set of consultants acted as 'centaurs', like the mythical half-horse, half-human creature, dividing and delegating their solution-creation activities to the AI or to themselves. Another set of consultants acted more like 'cyborgs', completely integrating their task flow with the AI and continually interacting with the technology.

The overall results suggest that AI will have a large impact on work, one which will increase with language models' capabilities, but the impacts will be uneven. The authors suggest that the capabilities of AI create a 'jagged technological frontier', where some tasks are easily done by AI, while others, though seemingly similar in difficulty level, are outside the current capability of AI (Dell'Acqua et al., 2023).

It can be concluded that different technologies, digital online platforms as workplaces, and digitalisation of work generally based on human decisions have context-related specific impacts on task and job content and work structures, and through them on human work activities and their outcomes. The decisions to implement and use digital innovations such as AI can:

- *Replace and destroy tasks and jobs* by removing human labour in work processes. For example, three-dimensional (3D) printing replaces some phases and human operations in manufacturing processes; and AI algorithms replace some cognitive functions.
- *Hybridise tasks and jobs* by adding new job demands and features to them – for example, medical diagnosis by a cardiologist with the help of AI – leading to enriched and hybrid jobs, 'cobotisation', partly new competencies, new constituents in competencies, and renewed job descriptions, for example, digital marketer.
- *Create new tasks and jobs* by adding new job demands and reallocating jobs, for example, work in social media or advisors in virtual worlds.

Models of Hybrid Work

Some scenarios have been presented after the pandemic regarding hybrid work and its development. Kauffeld et al. (2022) identified these using the Delphi technique and generated 35 work scenarios and their characteristics, and categorised them. On the organisational level, positive developments are expected regarding technology, for example, advances in virtuality and artificial intelligence; and leadership, for example, increases in shared leadership and participation. On the individual level, the work–life integration of employees – for example, more flexibility and self-management – was considered important in the future. Negative effects were seen for teamwork regarding social relations: for example, building and maintaining team cohesion and social exchange becomes more difficult.

Several hybrid work models are available considering the implementation from the individual, team and organisational levels. Available models mostly describe hybrid work as a work arrangement where an employee divides their time between working at a traditional main workplace, and working remotely from another location (Barrero et al., 2021), with a lack of attention to other elements of HW. As examples of individual-level models, Kauffeld et al.

(2022) suggest a balanced mix of mobile and face-to-face work as an ideal prospective work model for most workers at the present time. Hopkins and Bardoel (2023) suggest five types: (1) full-time remote; (2) full-time office workers; (3) office frequency and days both fixed; (4) fixed office frequency, but attendance days flexible; and (5) fully flexible: workers choose the location where they work and when. The authors also state that whatever work arrangement is adopted, support for the mission and operations of the organisation is needed. Also, establishing and maintaining an aligned workplace culture is important, and ways of communication must be ensured. In addition, focusing on the health and well-being of employees and their skills and competencies is required. Appropriate technology and infrastructure are needed to support these activities. As an example, a team-level model of Smite et al. (2023, p. 40) defines hybrid teams 'with members altering their office days and WFA [working from anywhere] days in an erratic manner, followed by a spectrum of partially aligned options, in which not all team members and/or not always have the level playing field work experiences' (Box 9.2). On the organisational level, there will be organisations who uses a mixture of the above-described individual- and team-level arrangements based on their vision, goals, products, and needs.

BOX 9.2 AN EXAMPLE OF FUTURE TEAM MODELS

An example of a hybrid team model is the one presented by Smite et al. (2023, p. 36) in their team typology concerning software teams. They consider the location (where the work is performed) and work schedule (when the work is performed) to be the relevant core dimensions for understanding individual work arrangements in the future workplace. They add a third important dimension that distinguishes flexible work arrangements in the team context: the degree of alignment of the individual arrangements among the team members. Based on these dimensions, they propose a team typology.

The traditional on-site teams with aligned work schedules will prevail in the future, as well as *permanent multilocational remote teams*, with members working from different geographically distant offices of the same or different cooperating companies. *Variegated teams* change or variegate their team's work arrangement between the office and remote locations. These teams have predefined but changing work locations, with varying degrees of office presence. *Partially aligned teams* surface when not everybody's arrangements are aligned, or when members do not always align. *Hybrid teams* are related to distributed teams, but instead of office locations, their members can work from anywhere, having an erratic office presence. Additionally, they can be partially aligned (or partially hybrid) teams.

What comes to the work schedule, teams have three options: (1) *overlapping work hours*, for example, 9 a.m.–5 p.m.; (2) *flexible mode* with potentially erratic work schedule; and (3) *partially aligned* work schedules: either core hours mode with designed time overlaps, in which members choose a synchronisation window and have otherwise flexible schedules; or core meeting mode organised around scheduled meetings or designed events, which members agree to attend planned meetings, gatherings and events, but otherwise keep work schedules flexible (Smite et al., 2023, pp. 34–41).

FUTURE DEVELOPMENT OF SPACES

HW, as a flexible way of organising work, has many manifestations. During the pandemic, hybrid work's expected elements, sub-elements and features were much discussed. However, we do not yet know the functionalities and outcomes of different combinations of hybridity, although experiences of past remote and telework, virtual teams, and working from home during the pandemic, show the developmental trends. Therefore, job profiling is needed. That is, tasks need to be delineated into those best performed on site and remotely, and then those tasks need to be coordinated. Table 9.1 shows some features to consider when designing a hybrid work unit.

There is a need to cluster, measure and evaluate hybrid work outcomes, even though they are heterogeneous. What common indicators can be used? A reality test of implemented HW solutions could provide a starting point to consider various indicators. The basic elements, sub-elements and features used should be described in each case. In addition, data should include information about organisational values, purpose and goals; individual needs; job demands and available resources; performance and well-being outcomes on the individual, team and organisation levels. Based on this kind of information, conclusions for team- and organisation-level agreements can be established and refined, as can the need for relevant regulation and legislation.

Physical Spaces in the Future

Physical space refers to places where you work, live and spend other time. People always locate in some physical place and environment. Harrison and Dourish (1996, p. 69) suggested that 'Space is the opportunity; place is the understood reality … We are located in "space", but we act in "place".' From the work viewpoint, physical premises and environments enable performing in workplaces.

Table 9.1 The hybrid work 'sandwich table'

<table>
<tr><th rowspan="2">ELEMENTS AND SUB-ELEMENTS</th><th rowspan="2">INFLEX-IBILITY</th><th colspan="20">FEATURES OF HYBRIDITY</th><th rowspan="2">FULL FLEX-IBILITY</th></tr>
<tr><th colspan="7">Low flexibility</th><th colspan="6">Medium flexibility</th><th colspan="7">High flexibility</th></tr>
<tr><td>PHYSICAL
• Locations and workplaces</td><td>On site</td><td colspan="4">Main workplace</td><td colspan="4">Home</td><td colspan="4">Other places</td><td colspan="4">Third places</td><td colspan="4">Moving places</td><td>Many, anywhere, remote</td></tr>
<tr><td>• Mobility</td><td>Fixed place</td><td colspan="4">Campus mobility</td><td colspan="4">Pendulum</td><td colspan="4">Yo-Yo</td><td colspan="4">Nomads</td><td colspan="4">Carriers</td><td>Digital mobility</td></tr>
<tr><td rowspan="2">VIRTUAL
• Asynchronous
• Synchronous</td><td rowspan="2">Tools for solo use</td><td colspan="20">Tools and applications for knowledge search, processing, communication and collaboration</td><td rowspan="2">Digital ecosystem for all</td></tr>
<tr><td colspan="5">Information and knowledge management, e.g., documents</td><td colspan="5">Communication, e.g., email, videoconferencing</td><td colspan="5">Support and sharing, e.g., calendar, GDrive</td><td colspan="5">Collaboration, e.g., platforms, virtual worlds, metaverse</td></tr>
<tr><td rowspan="2">SOCIAL
• Communication
• Social relations
• Task-oriented
• Group maintenance</td><td rowspan="2">Entirely in-person, solo work</td><td colspan="4">Face-to-face with few or many</td><td colspan="4">Working synchronously and asynchronously online with another</td><td colspan="4">Working synchronously and asynchronously online with few or many</td><td colspan="4">Working face-to-face, AND synchronously and asynchronously online with few or many</td><td colspan="4">Working face-to-face in many places, AND synchronously and asynchronously online with few or many</td><td rowspan="2">All dispersed, group work</td></tr>
<tr><td colspan="5">Relations with colleagues, superiors, customers, family, friends</td><td colspan="5">Knowledge sharing concerning tasks, cooperation, and coordination</td><td colspan="5">Team-building for developing trust and cohesion</td><td colspan="5">Communication and collaboration in ad hoc team</td></tr>
</table>

ELEMENTS AND SUB-ELEMENTS	INFLEXIBILITY	FEATURES OF HYBRIDITY			FULL FLEXIBILITY
		Low flexibility	Medium flexibility	High flexibility	
TEMPORAL • How long • When • How often	Externally regulated	Fixed full-time or part-time	Agreed flexible time	Individual time	Self-regulated
		Never – rarely - sometimes – very often - always			
DECISION POWER	Control	Work methods – work schedule – decision-making – location autonomy – work-task autonomy			Autonomy
		Employer – manager/supervisor – team - worker			

OUTCOME
DILEMMAS

MENTAL SPACE	'One-size-for-all'	Physical premises: multifunctional office vs. remote working conditions Transport: savings in commuting time vs. travelling due to leisure activities Human-technology: technostress, fatigue, data security vs. communication and collaboration enabler Social relations: social isolation, loneliness, decreased collaboration vs. ability to concentrate, family support Gender equality: increased workload vs. flexibility in managing things Communication paradox: constant availability vs. 'right to disconnect' Work–family: blurring of work and personal life vs. relaxation, support, recovery Autonomy paradox: increased workload vs. sustainable autonomy Health and well-being: poor ergonomics, physical immobility, health complaints vs. self-determined pauses, recovery Leadership: monitoring vs. trust …….	Flexibility
PERFORMANCE	Added value	Nature of tasks (i.e., complexity), low-intensity telework, contents of social interaction moderate the impact	Sustainability

The main challenges during the pandemic concerned inconvenient working conditions when working from home; their ergonomic quality was poor. Furnishing home offices and other places with office equipment was costly. Premises in the office were half-empty, and after the pandemic, did not always support socialising and creative action.

In future hybrid work, flexible and smart physical workplaces are needed in different locations. This implicates the integration of physical and virtual spaces. The variety of using different locations and workplaces will increase. This emphasises the importance of the physical quality of each workplace. An employee can be independent of location, but still dependent on the quality of their workplace. For example, a digital nomad is a specific type of location-independent worker. Working from anywhere opens the door to complete temporal and spatial flexibility. On the other hand, looking for and finding operative working conditions with infrastructures can be challenging, as well as scheduling work with distant others, and the quality of social and mental spaces can be poor. Potential locations of workplaces in hybrid work include (Vartiainen, 2007, p. 29): (1) the employee's home; (2) the main workplace (the employer's premises); (3) vehicles, such as cars, buses, trams, trains, planes and ships; (4) a customer's or partner's premises, or an alternative premises of the company ('other workplaces'); and (5) hotels, cafés, parks, and so on ('third workplaces'). Each workplace, wherever it is, features its spatial organisation (for example, size and shape), architectonic details (for example, materials and colours), office or work station views (for example, what is seen from an adjacent workspace), and other workplace resources (for example, equipment, impact on work fluency). Mobility of the staff is closely related to the locations, and using them. Locations and mobility as the sub-elements of physical space can be used for profiling hybrid workers. In profiling, the features of locations (for example, whether there is a default workplace to return to), and temporal features (for example, the frequency of location changes), can be used. Each type of mobile work has its basic physical space and time criteria. 'On-site movers' work in a limited work area, 'yo-yos' return to a main office, 'pendulums' have two recurrent work locations, 'nomads' work in more than two places, and 'carriers' cannot do their work at a fixed location and must work while moving (Lilischkis, 2003).

Virtual Spaces of the Future

A virtual space is a digital layer of an environment in which individuals and groups work and collaborate. Dispersed virtual workplaces are needed when employees move a lot, work wherever they are, and collaborate from there. This means a varied digital tool option depending on the type of hybrid work. Due to recent and future developments in information and communication technologies, the domains of social and material worlds are not distinct and independent spheres of organisational life, but are mixed. For example, online communities can offer full-time flexible workers a 'digital third place' for socialising and making friends.

The main challenges during the pandemic were related to the shortcomings in some technological features – for example, how to record a meeting – and in the competencies to use technologies. The collaboration networks of workers became more static and siloed, with fewer bridges between disparate parts. The high frequency, duration and burstiness of online meetings resulted in a higher level of fatigue experienced, and the fatigue was associated with negative attitudes towards meetings. In all, the technostress was shown as 'Zoom fatigue' or, more generally 'videoconference fatigue'. The reasons for fatigue return to a communication medium's naturalness; that is, its lack.

In hybrid work, there are great expectations concerning developing richer virtual working environments. Tools are needed for different purposes – that is, information and data search, processing, communication and collaboration – as well as for various situations: that is, when working with others asynchronously and sometimes synchronously on site and alone independently from any place. To create favourable virtual spaces, a set of fundamental technologies are needed. The infrastructure enables digital connectivity for hybrid workers to send and receive data, information and knowledge. Services and applications are needed for performing task-related operations and actions, and co-working. As the expectation is that hybrid work takes place from different locations and workplaces, in both solo and cooperative modes, individual workers need autonomous tools – for example, laptops and smartphones – as well as collaboration platforms, for example for meetings. The role of AI as a cognitive workmate of humans is expected to add a new technological feature to the working environment.

The limitations of many available platforms were described above, showing their unnaturalness. *Virtual worlds* as communication and collaboration platforms can offer a richer environment with various tools enabling rich real-time communication. In these, multiple actors share the same three-dimensional digital space, despite occupying remote physical locations. It is possible to navigate and manipulate objects there, and communicate with one another via *avatars* that are flexible and easily transformed digital self-representations in a graphic 3D form (Yee and Bailenson, 2007). Virtual worlds and their affordances provide platforms for different purposes. Some of the most common uses are small business meetings for negotiations and decision-making, or meetings for product ideation and design. In particular, virtual worlds may be able to support the creative collaboration and innovation that research shows are critical to many organisations. One strength of virtual world environments is the ability to use parallel communication tools. For example, users can chat, talk, write and work. The benefits of virtual worlds are very similar to the advantages of other online collaboration technologies. For example, they can lower travel costs, provide access from anywhere with an Internet connection, and contribute to rather strong feelings of presence and visibility. In addition, they can be tailored to an organisation's specific needs.

The *metaverse* is expected to be the next phase of collaboration platforms integrating physical reality, augmented reality (AR) and virtual reality (VR). It is used for different purposes, one of them being supporting synchronous and asynchronous collaboration. As platforms, they are fully digital, engaging and mutually fitting virtual worlds that can be used flexibly. Dwivedi et al. (2022, p. 2) describe the metaverse as: 'the layer between you and reality', and as a '3D virtual shared world where all activities can be carried out with the help of augmented and virtual reality services'. The metaverse provides a sociomaterial context for working by enabling social practices in a developed technological platform. Possibly in the future, as the metaverse continues to grow, entities in the physical world, such as cities and companies, will establish virtual versions of themselves. When knowledge-based work objects and work processes are transformed into digital twins, it is possible to recruit workers to earn their living in them.

Social Spaces of the Future

Social spaces refer to other people in work and life that form social contexts and relations of hybrid workers, both face-to-face and online. In the workplace, other people include colleagues, co-workers, superiors and management, and clients. The family sphere consists of partners, children, relatives and friends. Social space itself has become a hybrid of face-to-face and virtual interaction and collaboration, especially due to social media.

The main social challenges during the pandemic were professional and social isolation and feelings of loneliness, a potential reduction in chances of promotion, and a reduction in intra-organisational communication and technical support. Social isolation was shown in missing colleagues, challenges in trust and the quality of remote leadership, and in blurring work and life at home.

It can be expected that the social space and relations will become even more complicated than before. In hybrid work, virtual and physical spaces overlap in the social spaces that are used as the context for interactions. For example, in the extreme case of mobile work, an employee may need to organise a series of face-to-face meetings with employees at each location and communicate simultaneously online synchronously and asynchronously with many people (Figure 9.2).

Types of communication and collaboration events

Presence	Social absence	Social presence	Virtual presence	Dual presence	Multi-presence
Physical place	Yes	Yes	Yes	Yes, in one place	Yes, in changing places
Face-to-face with other(s)	No	Yes	No	Yes	Yes: many
Mediated/ virtual	No	No	Online with other(s)	Online with other(s)	Online + asynchronously with other(s)

Source: Based on Koroma and Vartiainen (2018, p. 193).

Figure 9.2 Different types of presence in hybrid work

Communication and collaboration events follow each other and are divided into five types depending on the type of space and the method of communication used. The events take place in different and changing circumstances and are influenced by the technology in use, the local context and situational demands. Some events are meant for working alone *without social contact*, and other events have *others present* face-to-face. The third type of event occurs when other(s) are *virtually present* online. A *dual presence* is needed when a social event occurs both face-to-face and online with others. The *multipresent* event occurs when an individual works virtually by simultaneously using different synchronous and asynchronous technologies in a physical place that is also occupied by other people. Mobile information and communication technology (mICT) does not bind a user to one physical place, but instead it is possible to maintain a virtual presence and availability while changing physical and social environments. Multipresence enlarges the concept of presence and dual presence by including simultaneous synchronic and asynchronic communication, using different technologies in changing locations. In practice, the multipresence is shown as increased job demands and well-being outcomes. The technology-enabled multipresence concept defines workers' preference to be simultaneously present in physical, virtual and social spaces, while working across boundaries in multiple locations and on the move. States of presence arise from different combinations of physical, virtual and social spaces ranging from absence to presence, both socially and virtually. In the future, the virtual world environments as imitations of 'real world' may make social relations easier to manage.

Mental Space

The mental space refers to the cognitive-emotional structure and processes of the human mind. Information and knowledge from the working environments are collected and reflected in mental space, interpreted as cognitions and affective states, and used to regulate work activities. The human mind in mental space has two main functions: initiating actions, and reflecting their outcomes. The above-described space elements, sub-elements, and their features impact upon how the work is experienced in hybrid work.

The main challenges of mental space as the outcomes of remote and teleworking were the controversial and dilemmatic experiences during the pandemic. There were feelings of social isolation, increased workload, constant connectivity, gender inequality, technostress, missing competencies, deteriorating physical health and well-being. However, on the other hand, many positive experiences and feelings were related to the increased autonomy.

In hybrid work, the outcomes of hybrid work can be used as the criteria to evaluate how well the implementation of new ways of working has succeeded. The main efforts should be concentrated to strengthen the benefits identified in remote and telework studies, such as ways to balance work and life, to find a suitable level of autonomy. On the other hand, the efforts could also concentrate on overcoming the existing controversies, for example, solving the autonomy and communication paradoxes, work–life balance, and control-based versus trust-based leadership,

HYBRID WORK CONCEPT AND FRAMEWORK

The main conclusion of this book is that hybrid work is many-faced and can be realised by combining work elements in a flexible manner. Etymologically, 'hybrid' refers to something formed by combining two or more things. Because so many things are made up of two or more things, especially because the interest is in looking at the potential of hybrid work, this book uses the concept only in individual work, workplaces and organisations. A hybrid work entity is formed by combining two or more things to act resiliently in both stable and turbulent environments and situations. Based on the conceptual analysis, it was suggested in the theoretical introduction that the 'two or more things' in hybrid work and workplaces are the four basic elements of physical, virtual/digital, social and temporal spaces. These elements are interconnected, each having sub-elements and adjustable features. However, the content analysis of the remote work and telework literature, HW definitions in the literature and country reports, and of debates on these subjects and the expected demands and resources during the pandemic, showed that many new features were available for use when designing and implementing hybrid work in practice.

The hybrid work definitions in the literature and country reports during the pandemic typically referenced only location and temporal elements. This is also common today, in the year 2024. The comparison with the concepts used in earlier remote work and telework definitions shows that the elements are similar, though in a more compact form, and with different weights. For example, the European Framework Agreement's (ETUC et al., 2002) definition of telework includes physical space (location), virtual space (information and communication technology, ICT) and temporal (time frequency) elements, in addition to referring to the need for an employment contract or relationship as a feature. Later, in the definition of telework and ICT-based mobile work (Eurofound, 2020, p. 1), physical space (excluding the main workplace) and virtual space (ICT) elements, in addition to being a feature of flexible arrangements, were used. The virtual element has played only a minor role in the definitions of hybrid work during the pandemic, although growing later. The definitions have been reminiscent of 'classic' definitions of telework and ICT-based mobile work, although they included virtuality. The social element still seemed to be missing, despite being part of the discussion regarding challenges and opportunities.

It can be concluded that 'old' remote work and telework are also types of hybrid work. For example, traditional telework combines certain physical, temporal and virtual elements and their features. It could thus be logically reasoned that other types of remote work and telework are just specific types of hybrid configurations, and even manual work can include hybrid elements; for example, an artisan might design their products using 3D design software, and manufacture them by hand at home. The potential for variety in hybrid work increases even more when considering hybridity at the team and organisational levels. A summary of hybrid remote work and telework on the individual level is provided in Box 9.3.

BOX 9.3 DEFINING HYBRID REMOTE AND TELEWORK

- *HW is a systemic entity*, and its type and form depend on the purpose of activities, the needs of actors, and their contextual demands and available resources (i.e., hindrances, challenges, benefits, and opportunities).
- *HW is built on basic elements, sub-elements and their features* on the individual, team, organisational and societal levels.
- *HW is a dynamic entity* transforming in time (see Figures 3.5a and 3.5b in Chapter 3) driven by changes in an actor's purpose, needs, context and resources. Stable conditions tend to freeze the HW configuration.

- *An individual-level formulation* of HW is as follows: hybrid work (HW) is any type of work arrangement where a worker operates in a sustainable manner alone or with others, as agreed upon by the worker and organisation, based on the latter's purpose, the former's needs and tasks, and the context, with flexibility regarding the time and place of the work – at the employer's premises or default location, or remotely at home, at other locations or on the road – using digital technologies such as laptops, mobile phones and the Internet.
  - *'Any type of work arrangement'* means that HW is any configuration of two or more basic elements and their sub-elements and features.
  - *'In a sustainable manner'* means that the work's purpose, the actors' needs, contextual and situational demands, and the available resources fit.
  - *'As agreed'* means that the identification of needed elements, sub-elements and features, as well as their design and implementation, are based on agreements and contracts between stakeholders on different levels (team, organisation, society).
  - *'Operates ... alone or with others'* means that an actor (individual, team or organisation) works independently and/or collaborates with other actors.
  - *'Based on the latter's purpose'* means that HW contributes to the organisation's purpose and goals when it produces products, provides services or generates knowledge.
  - *'Based on ... the former's needs and tasks, and the context'* means that HW accounts for the varying needs of an individual, which impact upon their motivation to do the tasks involved in their current context-dependent job demands.
  - *'With flexibility regarding the time and place of the work'* means that HW can make flexible use of time and location, including the workplace, as agreed between the stakeholders.
  - *'Using digital technologies'* means that technologies, including hardware and software, are used in HW to process and search for information and to collaborate.

NOTE

1. Across the Asia Pacific, 2170 leaders participated in the Hybrid Leadership survey from Australia and New Zealand, India, Indonesia, Japan, China, Malaysia, the Philippines, Singapore, South Korea, Sri Lanka, Thailand, Vietnam, and some other countries. In addition, 27 senior executives were interviewed.

References

Aksoy, C.G., Barrero, J.M., Bloom, N., Davis, S.J., Dolls, M., and Zarate, P. 2023. *Working from Home Around the Globe: 2023 Report*, EconPol Policy Brief, 53, July.

Akuoko, P.B., Aggrey, V., and Mengba, J.D. 2021. Mothering with a career during a pandemic: the case of the Ghanaian woman. *Gender, Work and Organization*, 28(S2): 277–288.

Alexander, A., Cracknell, R., De Smet, A., Langstaff, M., Mysore, M., and Ravid, D. 2021. *What Executives are Saying about the Future of Hybrid Work*, McKinsey Global Publishing.

Allen, T.D., Golden, T.D., and Shockley, K.M. 2015. How effective is telecommuting? Assessing the status of our scientific findings. *Psychological Science in the Public Interest*, 16(2): 40–68. https://doi.org/10.1177/1529100615593273.

Allen, T.D., Johnson, R.C., Kiburz, K.M., and Shockley, K.M. 2013. Work–family conflict and flexible work arrangements: deconstructing flexibility. *Personnel Psychology*, 66(2): 345–376. https://doi.org/10.1111/peps.12012.

Aloisi, A., and De Stefano, V. 2022. Essential jobs, remote work and digital surveillance: addressing the COVID-19 pandemic panopticon. *International Labour Review*, 161(2): 289–314.

Ancona, D., Bresman, H., and Mortensen, M. 2021. Shifting team research after COVID-19: evolutionary and revolutionary change. *Journal of Management Studies*, 58(1): 289–293.

Andreev, P., Salomon, I., and Pliskin, N. 2010. Review: state of teleactivities. *Transportation Research*, 18C(1): 3–20.

Andriessen, J.H.E. 2003. *Working with Groupware: Understanding and Evaluating Collaboration Technology*, Cham: Springer.

Andriessen, J.H.E., and Vartiainen, M. (eds) 2006. *Mobile Virtual Work – A New Paradigm*, Heidelberg: Springer-Verlag.

Arena, M.J., Carroll, G.R., O'Reilly, C.A., Golden, J., and Hines, S. 2022. The adaptive hybrid: innovation with virtual work. *Management and Business Review*, 2(1): 21–31.

Atkinson, J. 1984. Manpower strategies for flexible organisations. *Personnel Management*, 16, 28–31.

Avolio, B.J., Kahai, S., and Dodge, G.E. 2000. E-leadership: implications for theory, research, and practice. *Leadership Quarterly*, 11(4): 615–668. https://doi.org/10.1016/S1048-9843(00)00062-X.

Bailey, D.E., and Kurland, N.B. 2002. A review of telework research: findings, new directions, and lessons for the study of modern work. *Journal of Organizational Behavior: The International Journal of Industrial, Occupational and Organizational Psychology and Behavior*, 23(4): 383–400.

Bakker, A.B. 2011. An evidence-based model of work engagement. *Current Directions in Psychological Science*, 20(4): 265–269. https://doi.org/10.1177/0963721411414534.

Bakker, A.B., and Demerouti, E. 2017. Job demands–resources theory: taking stock and looking forward. *Journal of Occupational Health Psychology*, 22(3): 273–285.

Bakker, A.B., Breevaart, K., Scharp, Y.S., and de Vries, J.D. 2021. Daily self-leadership and playful work design: proactive approaches of work in times of crisis. *Journal of Applied Behavioral Science*, 1–23. https://doi.org/10.1177/00218863211060453.

Bakker, A., Hakanen, J.J., Demerouti, E., and Xanthopoulou, D. 2007. Job resources boost work engagement, particularly when job demands are high. *Journal of Educational Psychology*, 99(2): 274–284. https://doi.org/10.1037/0022–0663.99.2.274.

Barney, J.B. 1991. Firm resources and sustained competitive advantage. *Journal of Management*, 17(1): 99–120.

Barrero, J.M., Bloom, N., and Davis, S.J. 2021. *Why Working from Home Will Stick*, National Bureau of Economic Research Working Paper 28731. www.wfhresearch.com.

Bartsch, S., Weber, E., Büttgen, M., and Huber, A. 2020. Leadership matters in crisis-induced digital transformation: how to lead service employees effectively during the COVID-19 pandemic. *Journal of Service Management*, 32(1): 71–85. https://doi.org/10.1108/JOSM-05-2020-0160.

Beauregard, T.A., Basile, K.A., and Canonico, E. 2013. *Home is Where the Work Is: A New Study of Homeworking in Acas – And Beyond*, Research Paper 10, ACAS.

Beauregard, T.A., Basile, K.A., and Canónico, E. 2019. Telework: outcomes and facilitators for employees. In: Landers, R.N. (ed.), *The Cambridge Handbook of Technology and Employee Behavior*, Cambridge: Cambridge University Press, pp. 511–543.

Becker, F., and Sims, W. 2000. *Managing Uncertainty. Integrated Portfolio Strategies for Dynamic Organizations*, Ithaca, NY: Cornell University, International Workplace Studies Program.

Bell, B., and Kozlowski, S. 2002. A typology of virtual teams: implications for effective leadership. *Group and Organization Management*, 27(1): 14–49.

Bell, B.S., McAlpine, K.L., and Hill, N.S. 2023. Leading virtually. *Review of Organizational Psychology and Organizational Behavior*, 10(1): 339–362. Available at SSRN: https://ssrn.com/abstract=4337239 or http://dx.doi.org/10.1146/annurev-orgpsych-120920-050115.

Bentley, S.V., Haslam, C., Haslam, S.A., Jetten, J., Larwood, J., and La Rue, C.J. 2021. GROUPS 2 CONNECT: an online activity to maintain social connection and well-being during COVID-19. *Applied Psychology: Health and Well-Being*, 1–22. doi: 10.1111/aphw.12330.

Berg, J., Furrer, M., Harmon, E., Rani, U., and Silberman, M.S. 2018. *Digital Labour Platforms and the Future of Work: Towards Decent Work in the Online World*, Geneva: International Labour Office.

Bergmann, R., Rintel, S., Baym, N., Sarkar, A., Borowiec, D., Wong, P., and Sellen, A. 2023. Meeting (the) pandemic: videoconferencing fatigue and evolving tensions of sociality in enterprise video meetings during COVID-19. *Computer Supported Cooperative Work*, 32, 347–383. https://doi.org/10.1007/s10606-022-09451-6.

Bernardino, A.F., Roglio, K.D.D., and Del Corso, J.M. 2012. Telecommuting and HRM: a case study of an information technology service provider. *JISTEM – Journal of Information Systems and Technology Management*, 9(2): 285–306.

Besharov, M., and Mitzinneck, B. 2020. Heterogeneity in organizational hybridity: a configurational, situated, and dynamic approach. In: Besharov, M., and Mitzinneck, B. (eds), *Organizational Hybridity: Perspectives, Processes, Promises*

(Research in the Sociology of Organizations, Vol. 69), Bingley: Emerald Group Publishing, pp. 3–25.
Biron, M., and Van Veldhoven, M. 2016. When control becomes a liability rather than an asset: comparing home and office days among part-time teleworkers. *Journal of Organizational Behavior*, 37(8): 1317–1337.
Blackburn, R.S., Furst, S.A., and Rosen, B. 2003. Building a winning virtual team. In: Gibson, C. and Cohen, S. (eds), *Virtual Teams that Work: Creating Conditions for Effective Virtual Teams*, San Francisco, CA: Jossey, pp. 95–120.
Blomberg, A.J., and Kallio, T.J. 2022. A review of the physical context of creativity: a three-dimensional framework for investigating the physical context of creativity. *International Journal of Management Reviews*, 24(3): 433–451. https://doi.org/10.1111/ijmr.12286.
Blomqvist, K., Sivunen, A., Vartiainen, M., Olsson, T., Ropponen, A., Henttonen, A., and Van Zoonen, W. 2020. *Remote Work in Finland during the Covid-19 Pandemic: Results of a Longitudinal Study*. https://futuremote.fi/wp-content/uploads/2020/12/Remote-work-in-Finland-during-the-Covid-19-pandemic.pdf.
Bloom, N., Han, R., and Liang, J. 2022. *How Hybrid Working from Home Works Out*, Working Paper 30292, Cambridge, MA: National Bureau of Economic Research. http://www.nber.org/papers/w30292.
Bloom, N., Liang, J., Roberts, J., and Ying, Z.J. 2014. Does working from home work? Evidence from a Chinese experiment. *Quarterly Journal of Economics*, 130(1): 165–218.
Boell, S.K., Campbell, J., Cecez-Kecmanovic, D., and Cheng, J.E. 2013. The transformative nature of telework: a review of the literature. In: *Proceedings of the 19th Americas Conference on Information Systems*, Chicago, IL.
Boutellier, R., Ullman, F., Schreiber, J., and Naef, R. 2008. Impact of office layout on communication in a science-driven business. *R&D Management*, 38(4): 372–391.
Brown, S.G., Hill, N., and Lorinkova, N.M. 2021. Leadership and virtual team performance: a meta-analytic investigation. *European Journal of Work and Organizational Psychology*, 30(5): 672–685. https://doi.org/10.1080/1359432X.2021.1914719.
Brucks, M.S., and Levav, J. 2022. Virtual communication curbs creative idea generation. *Nature*, 605: 108–112. https://doi.org/10.1038/s41586-022-04643-y.
Buecker, S., and Horstmann, K.T. 2021. Loneliness and social isolation during the COVID-19 pandemic: a systematic review enriched with empirical evidence from a large-scale diary study. *European Psychologist*, 26(4): 272–284.
Camacho, S., and Barrios, A. 2022. Teleworking and technostress: early consequences of a COVID-19 lockdown. *Cognition, Technology and Work*, 24(3): 441–457.
Carillo, K., Cachat-Rosset, G., Marsan, J., Saba, T., and Klarsfeld, A. 2021. Adjusting to epidemic-induced telework: empirical insights from teleworkers in France. *European Journal of Information Systems*, 30(1): 69–88.
Carsten, M., Goswami, A., Shepard, A., and Donnelly, L.I. 2021. Followership at a distance: follower adjustment to distal leadership during COVID-19. *Applied Psychology*. https://doi.org/10.1111/apps.12337.
Cavanaugh, M.A., Boswell, W.R., Roehling, M.V., and Boudreau, J.W. 2000. An empirical examination of self-reported work stress among U.S. managers. *Journal of Applied Psychology*, 85(1): 65–74.
Charalampous, M., Grant, C.A., Tramontano, C., and Michailidis, E. 2019. Systematically reviewing remote e-workers' well-being at work: a multidimensional approach. *European Journal of Work and Organizational Psychology*, 28(1): 51–73.

Choudhury, P. 2022. Geographic mobility, immobility, and geographic flexibility: a review and agenda for research on the changing geography of work. *Academy of Management Annals*, 16(1): 258–296. https://doi.org/10.5465/annals.2020.0242

Choudhury, P., Crowston, K., Dahlander, L., Minervini, M.S., and Raghuram, S. 2020. GitLab: work where you want, when you want. *Journal of Organization Design*, 9(1): 23.

Choudhury, P., Khanna, T., Makridis, C.A., and Schirmann, K. 2022. *Is Hybrid Work the Best of Both Worlds? Evidence from a Field Experiment*, Harvard Business School Working Paper, No. 22-063, March.

Chung, H. 2022. *The Flexibility Paradox – Why Flexible Working Leads to (Self-) Exploitation*, Bristol: Bristol University Press.

Claessens, B.J.C., van Eerde, W., Rutte, C.G., and Roe, R.A. 2007. A review of the time management literature. *Personnel Review*, 36(2): 255–276.

Contreras, F., Baykal, E., and Abid, G. 2020. E-leadership and teleworking in times of COVID-19 and beyond: what we know and where do we go. *Frontiers in Psychology*, 11: 590271. https://doi.org/10.3389/fpsyg.2020.590271.

Costa, P., Graça, A.M., Santos, C., Marques-Quinteiro, P., and Rico, R. 2021. Teamworking virtually: business as usual? *European Journal of Work and Organizational Psychology*, 30(5): 619–623. https:// doi .org/ 10 .1080/ 1359432X .2021.1936503.

Crandall, N.F., and Wallace, M.J. 1997. Inside the virtual workplace: forging a new deal for work and rewards. *Compensation and Benefits Review*, 29(1): 27–36. https:// doi.org/10.1177/088636879702900105.

Crawford, E.R., LePine, J.A., and Rich, B.L. 2010. Linking job demands and resources to employee engagement and burnout: a theoretical extension and meta-analytic test. *Journal of Applied Psychology*, 95(5): 834–848.

Crummenerl, C., Perronet, C., Ravindranath, S., Paolini, S., Lamothe, I., Schastok, I., Aggarwal, G., and Chakraborty, A. 2020. *The Future of Work: From Remote to Hybrid*, Capgemini Research Institute. www.capgemini.com/researchinstitute/.

Deci, E.L., and Ryan, R.M. 2012. Self-determination theory. In: Van Lange, P.A.M., Kruglanski, A.W., and Higgins, E.T. (eds), *Handbook of Theories of Social Psychology* (Vol. 1), Thousand Oaks, CA: SAGE, pp. 416–437.

Delaporte, I., and Peña, W. 2020. *Working from Home under COVID-19: Who is Affected? Evidence from Latin American and Caribbean Countries*, GLO Discussion Paper, No. 528, Essen: Global Labor Organization (GLO).

Dell'Acqua, F., McFowland III, E., Mollick, E., Lifshitz-Assaf, H., Kellogg, K.C., Rajendran, S., Krayer, L., Candelon, F., and Lakhani, K.R. 2023. *Navigating the Jagged Technological Frontier: Field Experimental Evidence of the Effects of AI on Knowledge Worker Productivity and Quality*, Working Paper 24-013, Harvard Business School.

de Menezes, L.M., and Kelliher, C. 2011. Flexible working and performance: a systematic review of the evidence for a business case. *International Journal of Management Reviews*, 13(4): 452–474.

Demerouti, E., Bakker, A.B., Nachreiner, F., and Schaufeli, W.B. 2001. The job demands–resources model of burnout. *Journal of Applied Psychology*, 86(3): 499–512. doi:10.1037/0021-9010.86.3.499.

Derks, D., van Duin, D., Tims, M., and Bakker, A.B. 2015. Smartphone use and work–home interference: the moderating role of social norms and employee work engagement. *Journal of Occupational and Organizational Psychology*, 88(1): 155–177.

De Vincenzi, C., Pansini, M., Ferrara, B., Buonomo, I., and Benevene, P. 2022. Consequences of COVID-19 on employees in remote working: challenges, risks and opportunities. An evidence-based literature review. *International Journal of Environmental Research and Public Health*, 19: 11672. https:// doi.org/ 10.3390/ ijerph191811672.

Dingel, J.I., and Neiman, B. 2020. How many jobs can be done at home? *Journal of Public Economics*, 189(2): 104235. https://doi.org/10.1016/j.jpubeco.2020.104235.

Duchek, S. 2020. Organizational resilience: a capability-based conceptualization. *Business Research*, 13(1): 215–246.

Dunn, M., Munoz, I., and Jarrahi, M.H. 2023. Dynamics of flexible work and digital platforms: task and spatial flexibility in the platform economy. *Digital Business*, 3(1): 100052. https://doi.org/10.1016/j.digbus.2022.100052.

Dwivedi, Y.K., Hughes, L., Baabdullah, A.M., Ribeiro-Navarrete, S., Giannakis, M., Al-Debei, M.M., Dennehy, D., Metri, B., Buhalis, D., Cheung, C.M., Conboy, K., Doyle, R., Dubey, R., Dutot, V., Felix, R., Goyal, D., Gustafsson, A., Hinsch, C., Jebabli, I., … Wamba, S.F. 2022. Metaverse beyond the hype: multidisciplinary perspectives on emerging challenges, opportunities, and agenda for research, practice and policy. *International Journal of Information Management*, 66: 102542. https:// doi.org/10.1016/j.ijinfomgt.2022.102542.

Edwards, J.R. 2008. Person–environment fit in organizations: an assessment of theoretical progress. *Academy of Management Annals*, 2(1): 167–230. doi:10.5465/19416520802211503, ISSN 1941-6520.

Ellingrud, K., Sanghvi, S., Singh Dandona, G., Madgavkar, A., Chui, M., White, O., and Hasebe, P. 2023. *Generative AI and the Future of Work in America*, Report, 26 July, McKinsey Global Institute. www.mckinsey.com/mgi.

Emery, F., and Trist, E. 1997 [1963]. The causal texture of organizational environments. In: Trist, E., Emery, F., and Murray, H. (eds), *The Social Engagement of Social Science: A Tavistock Anthology, vol. III: The Socio-Ecological Perspective*, Philadelphia, PA: University of Pennsylvania Press, pp. 53–65.

Engeström, Y., Rantavuori, P., Ruutu, P., and Tapola-Haapala, M. 2022. The hybridisation of adolescents' worlds as a source of developmental tensions: a study of discursive manifestations of contradictions, *Educational Review*. DOI: 10.1080/00131911.2022.2033704.

ETUC, UNICE/UEAPME and CEEP. 2002. *European Framework Agreement on Telework*. https:// resourcecentre .etuc .org/ sites/ default/ files/ 2020 -09/ Telework %202002_Framework%20Agreement%20-%20EN.pdf.

Eurofound. 2015. *New Forms of Employment*, Luxembourg: Publications Office of the European Union.

Eurofound. 2020. *Telework and ICT-Based Mobile Work: Flexible Working in the Digital Age* (New Forms of Employment series), Luxembourg: Publications Office of the European Union.

Eurofound. 2021. *Right to Disconnect: Exploring Company Practices*, Luxembourg: Publications Office of the European Union.

Eurofound. 2022. *The Rise in Telework: Impact on Working Conditions and Regulations*, Luxembourg: Publications Office of the European Union.

Eurofound. 2023. *Living and Working in Europe 2022*, Luxembourg: Publications Office of the European Union.

Eurofound and the International Labour Office. 2017. *Working Anytime, Anywhere: The Effects on the World of Work*, Luxembourg: Publications Office of the European Union; Geneva: International Labour Office. http://eurofound.link/ef1658.

European Framework on Telework. 2002. https://resourcecentre.etuc.org/sites/default/files/2020-09/Telework%202002_Framework%20Agreement%20-%20EN.pdf.

Fauville, G., Luo, M., Queiroz, A.C.M., Bailenson, J.N., and Hancock, J. 2021. Zoom exhaustion and fatigue scale. *Computers in Human Behavior*, Reports 4, 100119. https://doi.org/10.1016/j.chbr.2021.100119.

Felstead, A., and Henseke, G. 2017. Assessing the growth of remote working and its consequences for effort, well-being and work–life balance. *New Technology, Work and Employment*, 32(3): 195–212.

Felstead, A., Jewson, N., and Walters, S. 2005. *Changing Places of Work*, Basingstoke: Palgrave Macmillan.

Fernández-Macías, E., and Bisello, M. 2020. *A Taxonomy of Tasks for Assessing the Impact of New Technologies on Work*, JRC Working Papers Series on Labour, Education and Technology 2020/04, Seville: European Commission.

Fiol, C.M., and O'Connor, E.J. 2005. Identification in face-to-face, hybrid, and pure virtual teams: untangling the contradictions. *Organization Science*, 16(1): 19–32.

Fredrickson, B.L. 2001. The role of positive emotions in positive psychology: the broaden-and-build theory of positive emotions. *American Psychologist*, 56(3): 218–226.

Future of Jobs Report. 2023. *Insight Report*, May. World Economic Forum. https://www.weforum.org/reports/the-future-of-jobs-report-2023/.

Gajendran, R.S., and Harrison, D.A. 2007. The good, the bad, and the unknown about telecommuting: meta-analysis of psychological mediators and individual consequences. *Journal of Applied Psychology*, 92(6): 1524–1541.

Guidetti, G., Mazzei, E., Zappalà, S., and Toscano, F. 2021. Work from home during the COVID-19 outbreak: the impact on employees' remote work productivity, engagement, and stress. *Journal of Occupational Environmental Medicine*, 63(7): 426–443. doi:https://doi.org/10.1097/JOM.0000000000002236.

Ganguly, A., Joseph, J.M., Dutta, S., and Dey, K. 2022. Exploring the employer–employee relationship: a management versus employee perspective of the vicissitudes in the virtual workplace. *Global Business Review*. https://doi.org/10.1177/09721509221086353.

Gascoigne, C. 2021. *Flexible Working: Lessons from the Pandemic*, Chartered Institute of Personnel and Development (CIPD).

Gibbs, M., Mengel, F., and Siemroth, C. 2021. *Work from Home and Productivity: Evidence from Personnel and Analytics Data on IT Professionals*, Becker Friedman Institute for Economics Working Paper No. 2021-56, Chicago, IL: University of Chicago.

Gibbs, J.L., Sivunen, A., and Boyraz, M. 2017. Investigating the impacts of team type and design on virtual team processes. *Human Resource Management Review*, 27(4): 590–603.

Gibson, C.B., Gilson, L.L., Griffith, T.L., and O'Neill, T.A. 2023. Should employees be required to return to the office? *Organizational Dynamics*, 52(2): 100981. https://doi.org/10.1016/j.orgdyn.2023.100981.

Gilson, L., Maynard, M., Jones Young, N., Vartiainen, M., and Hakonen, M. 2015. Virtual teams research: 10 years, 10 themes and 10 opportunities. *Journal of Management*, 41(5): 1313–1337.

Giustiniano, L., Clegg, S.R., Cunha, M.P., and Rego, A. 2018. *Theories of Organizational Resilience*, Cheltenham, UK and Northampton, MA, USA: Edward Elgar Publishing.

Gohoungodji, P., N'Dri, A.B., and Matos, A.L.B. 2023. What makes telework work? Evidence of success factors across two decades of empirical research: a systematic and critical review. *International Journal of Human Resource Management*, 34(3): 605–649. DOI: 10.1080/09585192.2022.2112259.

Golden, T.D., and Fromen, A. 2011. Does it matter where your manager works? Comparing managerial work mode (traditional, telework, virtual) across subordinate work experiences and outcomes. *Human Relations*, 64(11): 451–475.

Golden, T.D., and Gajendran, R.S. 2019. Unpacking the role of a telecommuter's job in their performance: examining job complexity, problem solving, interdependence, and social support. *Journal of Business and Psychology*, 34(1): 55–69. https://doi.org/10.1007/s10869-018-9530-4.

Golden, T.D., and Raghuram, S. 2010. Teleworker knowledge sharing and the role of altered relational and technological interactions. *Journal of Organizational Behavior*, 31(8): 1061–1085.

Golden, T.G., and Veiga, J.F. 2008. The impact of superior–subordinate relationships on the commitment, job satisfaction, and performance of virtual workers. *Leadership Quarterly*, 19(1): 77–88.

Gonsalves, L. 2020. From face time to flex time: the role of physical space in worker temporal flexibility. *Administrative Science Quarterly*, 65(4): 1058–1091.

Gratton, L. 2021. How to do hybrid right? *Harvard Business Review*, May–June. https://hbr.org/2021/05/how-to-do-hybrid-right.

Greer, T.W., and Payne, S.C. 2014. Overcoming telework challenges: outcomes of successful telework strategies. *Psychologist-Manager Journal*, 17(2): 87–111.

Griffith, T.L., and Neale, M.A. 2001. Information processing in traditional, hybrid, and virtual teams: from nascent knowledge to transactive memory. In: Staw, B. and Sutton, R. (eds), *Research in Organizational Behavior*, Vol. 23, Stamford, CT: JAI Press, pp. 379–421. https://doi.org/10.1016/S0191-3085(01)23009-3.

Hacker, J., vom Brocke, J., Handali, J., Otto, M., and Schneider, J. 2020. Virtually in this together – how web-conferencing systems enabled a new virtual togetherness during the COVID-19 crisis. *European Journal of Information Systems*, 29(5): 563–584. DOI: 10.1080/0960085X.2020.1814680.

Hacker, W. 2021. *Psychische Regulation von Arbeitstätigkeiten 4.0*, vdf Hochschulverlag AG an der ETH Zürich.

Hackman, J.R. 2003. Learning more by crossing levels: evidence from airplanes, hospitals, and orchestras. *Journal of Organizational Behavior: The International Journal of Industrial, Occupational and Organizational Psychology and Behavior*, 24(8): 905–922.

Halford, S. 2005. Hybrid workspace: re-spatialisations of work, organisation and management. *New Technology, Work and Employment*, 29(1): 19–33.

Han, S.J., and Hazard, N. 2022. Shared leadership in virtual teams at work: practical strategies and research suggestions for human resource development. *Human Resource Development Review*, 21(3): 300–323. https://doi.org/10.1177/15344843221093376.

Harrison, S., and Dourish, P. 1996. Re-place-ing space: the roles of place and space in collaborative systems. In: *Proceedings of the 1996 ACM Conference on Computer Supported Cooperative Work*, pp. 67–76.

Hasan, H., and Kazlauskas, A. 2014. Activity theory: who is doing what, why and how. In: Hasan, H. (ed.), *Being Practical with Theory: A Window into Business Research*, Wollongong, Australia: THEORI, pp. 9–14.

Hatayama, M., Viollaz, M., and Winkler, H. 2020. *Jobs' Amenability to Working from Home: Evidence from Skills Surveys for 53 Countries*, Policy Research Working Paper No. 9241, World Bank.

Hill, E.J., Grzywacz, J.G., Allen, S., Blanchard, V.L., Matz-Costa, C., Shulkin, S., and Pitt-Catsouphes, M. 2008. Defining and conceptualizing workplace flexibility. *Community, Work and Family*, 11(2): 149–163.

Hislop, D., and Axtell, C. 2007. The neglect of spatial mobility in contemporary studies of work: the case of telework. *New Technology, Work and Employment*, 22(1): 34–51.

Hislop, D., and Axtell, C. 2009. To infinity and beyond? Workspace and multi-location worker. *New Technology, Work and Employment*, 24(1): 60–75.

Hobfoll, S.E. 1988. *The Ecology of Stress*, New York: Hemisphere Publishing Corp.

Hobfoll, S., Halbesleben, S., Neveu, J-P., and Westmen, M. 2018. Conservation of resources in the organizational context: the reality of resources and their consequences. *Annual Review of Organizational Psychology and Organizational Behavior*, 5: 103–128.

Holtham, C. 2008. Place and space strategies for 21st-century organizations. In: Wankel, C. (ed.), *21st Century Management: A Reference Handbook*, Thousand Oaks, CA: SAGE, pp. 451–460.

Hopkins, J., and Bardoel, A. 2023. The future is hybrid: how organisations are designing and supporting sustainable hybrid work models in post-pandemic Australia. *Sustainability*, 15: 3086. https:// doi.org/10.3390/su15043086.

Höddinghaus, M., Nohe, C., and Hertel, G. 2023. Leadership in virtual work settings: what we know, what we do not know, and what we need to do. *European Journal of Work and Organizational Psychology*. DOI: 10.1080/1359432X.2023.2250079.

Hyrkkänen, U., Vanharanta, O., Kuusisto, H., Polvinen, K., and Vartiainen, M. 2022. Predictors of job crafting in SMEs working in an ICT-based mobile and multilocational manner. *International Small Business Journal*. https:// doi .org/ 10 .1177/ 02662426221129157.

Illegems, V., and Verbeke, A. 2004. Telework: what does it mean for management? *Long Range Planning*, 37(4): 319–334.

ILO. 2020a. *Working from Home: Estimating the Worldwide Potential*, Policy Brief. https://www.ilo.org/wcmsp5/groups/public/---ed_protect/---protrav/---travail/documents/briefingnote/wcms_743447.pdf.

ILO. 2020b. *Defining Measuring Remote Work, Telework, Work at Home and Home-Based Work*, Policy Brief.

ILO. 2020c. *COVID-19: Guidance for Labour Statistics Data Collection*, 5 June, ILO Technical Note.

ILO. 2021a. *From Potential to Practice: Preliminary Findings on the Numbers of Workers Working from Home during the COVID-19 Pandemic*, Policy Brief.

ILO. 2021b. *How the COVID-19 Pandemic is Changing Business: A Literature Review*, Geneva: International Labour Organization.

ILO. 2021c. *Teleworking Arrangements during the COVID 19 Crisis and Beyond*, Paper prepared for the 2nd Employment Working Group Meeting under the 2021 Italian Presidency of the G20.

Ipsen, C., van Veldhoven, M., Kirchner, K., and Hansen, J.P. 2021. Six key advantages and disadvantages of working from home in Europe during COVID-19. *International Journal of Environmental Research and Public Health*, 18(4): 1826. https://doi.org/10.3390/ijerph18041826.

Jain, H., Padmanabhan, B., Pavlou, P.A., and Raghu, T.S. 2021. Editorial for the special section on humans, algorithms, and augmented intelligence: the future of work, organizations, and society. *Information Systems Research*, 32(3): 675–687. https://doi.org/10.1287/isre.2021.1046.

Kane, G.C., Nanda, R., Phillips, A.N., and Copulsky, J.R. 2021. *The Transformation Myth: Leading your Organization through Uncertain Times*, Cambridge, MA: MIT Press. DOI: 10.7551/mitpress/13965.001.0001.

Kauffeld, S., Tartler, D., Gräfe, H., and Windmann, A-K. 2022. What will mobile and virtual work look like in the future? Results of a Delphi-based study. *Gruppe. Interaktion. Organisation*, 53: 189–214. https://doi.org/10.1007/s11612-022-00627-8.

Kässi, O., and Lehdonvirta, V. 2018. Online labour index: measuring the online gig economy for policy and research. *Technological Forecasting and Social Change*, 137(C): 241–248.

Kässi, O., Lehdonvirta, V., and Stephany, F. 2021. *How Many Online Workers are there in the World? A Data-Driven Assessment*, Open Research Europe. https://doi.org/10.2139/ssrn.3810843.

Kelliher, C., and Anderson, D. 2010. Doing more with less? Flexible working practices and the intensification of work. *Human Relations*, 63(1): 83–106.

Koroma, J., and Vartiainen, M. 2018. From presence to multipresence: mobile knowledge workers' densified hours. In: Taylor, S., and Luckman, S. (eds), *The New Normal of Working Lives: Dynamics of Virtual Work*, Cham: Palgrave Macmillan, pp. 171–200. https://doi.org/10.1007/978-3-319-66038-7_9.

Korunka, C. (ed.) 2021. *Flexible Working Practices and Approaches – Psychological and Social Implications*, Cham: Springer International Publishing, pp. v–ix.

Kossek, E.E., and Lautsch, B.A. 2018. Work–life flexibility for whom? Occupational status and work–life inequality in upper, middle, and lower levels jobs. *Academy of Management Annals*, 12(1): 5–36. https://doi.org/10.5465/annals.2016.0059.

Kozlowski, S.W.J., Chao, G.T., and Van Fossen, J. 2021. Leading virtual teams. *Organization Dynamics*, 50(1): 1–11. https://doi.org/10.1016/j.orgdyn.2021.100842.

Kubicek, B., Prem, R., Baumgartner, V., Uhlig, L., and Korunka, C. 2021. Cognitive demands of flexible work. In: Korunka, C. (ed.), *Flexible Working Practices and Approaches – Psychological and Social Implications*, Cham: Springer International Publishing, pp. 19–37.

Kurland, N.B., and Cooper, C.D. 2002. Manager control and employee isolation in telecommuting environments. *Journal of High Technology Management Research*, 13(1): 107–126.

Lahti, E. 2019. Embodied fortitude: an introduction to the Finnish construct of sisu. *International Journal of Wellbeing*, 9(1): 61–82.

Lautsch, B.A., Kossek, E.E., and Eaton, S.C. 2009. Supervisory approaches and paradoxes in managing telecommuting implementation. *Human Relations*, 62(6): 795–827. https://doi.org/10.1177/0018726709104543.

Lazarus, R.S., and Folkman, S. 1984. *Stress Appraisal and Coping*, New York: Springer.

Leonardi, P.M., Treem, J.W., and Jackson, M.H. 2010. The connectivity paradox: using technology to both decrease and increase perceptions of distance in distributed work arrangements. *Journal of Applied Communication Research*, 38(1): 85–105.

Lewin, K. 1951. Defining the 'field at a given time'. In: Cartwright, D. (ed.), *Field Theory in Social Science: Selected Theoretical Papers*, New York: Harper-Row, pp. 43–59.

Lewin, K. 1972. Need, force and valence in psychological fields. In: Hollander, E.P., and Hunt, R.G. (eds), *Classic Contributions to Social Psychology*, Oxford: Oxford University Press, pp. 200–209.
Lewis, S. 2003. Flexible working arrangements: implementation, outcomes, and management. In: Cooper, C.L., and Robertson, T. (eds), *International Review of Industrial and Organizational Psychology 2003*, Volume 18, New York: Wiley, pp. 1–28. https://doi.org/10.1002/0470013346.ch1.
Lilischkis, S. 2003. *More Yo-Yos, Pendulums and Nomads: Trends of Mobile and Multi-Location Work in the Information Society* (STAR Issue Report No. 36), Empirica.
Lim, V.K.G., and Teo, T.S.H. 2022. Cyberloafing: a review and research agenda. *Applied Psychology. An International Review*. https://doi.org/10.1111/apps.12452.
Lipnack, J., and Stamps, J. 2000. *Virtual Teams: People Working Across Boundaries with Technology*, New York: Wiley & Sons.
Luthans, F. 2002. The need for and meaning of positive organizational behavior. *Journal of Organizational Behavior*, 23(6): 695–706.
Malhotra, A. 2021. The postpandemic future of work. *Journal of Management*, 47(5): 1091–1102. DOI: 10.1177/01492063211000435.
Martin, B.H., and MacDonnell, R. 2012. Is telework effective for organizations? A meta-analysis of empirical research on perceptions of telework and organizational outcomes. *Management Research Review*, 35(7): 602–616.
Martínez-Sánchez, A.M., Pérez-Pérez, M., de-Luis-Carnicer, P., and Vela-Jiménez, M.H. 2007a. Teleworking and workplace flexibility: a study of impact on firm performance. *Personnel Review*, 36(1): 42–64.
Martínez-Sánchez, A., Pérez-Pérez, M., De-Luis-Carnicer, P., and Vela-Jiménez, M. 2007b. Telework, human resource flexibility and firm performance. New Technology, Work and Employment, 22(3): 208–223.
Martínez-Sánchez, A., Pérez-Pérez, M., Vela-Jiménez, M.J., and de-Luis-Carnicer, P. 2008. Telework adoption, change management, and firm performance. *Journal of Organizational Change Management*, 21(1): 7–31.
Masuda, A.D., Poelmans,
S.A.Y., Allen, T.D., Spector, P.E., Lapierre, L.M., Cooper, C.L., Abarca, N., Brough, P., Ferreiro, P., Fraile, G., Lu, L., Lu, C-Q., Siu, O.L., O'Driscoll, M.P., Suarez Simoni, A., Shima, S., and Moreno-Velazquez, I. 2012. Flexible work arrangements availability and their relationship with work-to-family conflict, job satisfaction, and turnover intentions: A comparison of three country clusters. *Applied Psychology: An International Review*, 61(1): 1–29.
Mayo, M., Gomez-Mejia, L., Firfiray, S., Berrone, P., and Villena, V.H. 2016. Leader beliefs and CSR for employees: the case of telework provision. *Leadership and Organization Development Journal*, 37(5): 609–634.
Mazmanian, M., Orlikowski, W.J., and Yates, J. 2013. The autonomy paradox: the implications of mobile email devices for knowledge professionals. *Organization Science*, 24(5): 1337–1357.
McCarthy, A., Ahearne, A., Bohle-Carbonell, K., Ó Síocháin, T., and Deirdre, F. 2020. *Remote Working during COVID-19: Ireland's National Survey Initial Report*, Galway: National University of Ireland Galway, Whitaker Institute and Western Development Commission.
McCoy, J.M. 2005. Linking the physical work environment to creative context. *Journal of Creative Behavior*, 39(3): 169–192.

McNall, L.A., Masuda, A.D., and Nicklin, J.M. 2009. Flexible work arrangements, job satisfaction, and turnover intentions: the mediating role of work-to family enrichment. *Journal of Psychology*, 144(1): 61–81.

Mello, J.A. 2007. Managing telework programs effectively. *Employee Responsibilities and Rights Journal*, 19(4): 247–261.

Mokhtarian, P.L. 1991. *Defining Telecommuting (Research Report No. UCD-ITS-RR-91-04)*, Institute of Transportation Studies, University of California at Davis.

Morganson, V.J., Major, D.A., Oborn, K.L., Verive, J.M., and Heelan, M.P. 2010. Comparing telework locations and traditional work arrangements: differences in work–life balance support, job satisfaction, and inclusion. *Journal of Managerial Psychology*, 25(6): 578–595.

Morgeson, F.P., and Humphrey, S.E. 2006. The work design questionnaire (WDQ): developing and validating a comprehensive measure for assessing job design and the nature of work. *Journal of Applied Psychology*, 91(6): 1321–1339.

Morgeson, F.P., DeRue, D.S., and Karam, E.P. 2010. Leadership in teams: a functional approach to understanding leadership structures and processes. *Journal of Management*, 36(1): 5–39. https://doi.org/10.1177/0149206309347376.

Mourão, L., Costa, R.B., da Silva Abbad, G., Legentil, J., Martins, L.B., and Sandall, H. 2023. A short scale for managerial support to teleworkers. *Psico-USF*, 28(1): 165–177. DOI: 10.1590/1413-82712023280113.

Mutiganda, J.C., Wiitavaara, B., Heiden, M., Svensson, S., Fagerström, A., Bergström, G., and Aboagye, E. 2022. A systematic review of the research on telework and organizational economic performance indicators. *Frontiers in Psychology*, 13: 1035310.

Nilles, J.M. 1975. Telecommunications and organizational decentralization. *IEEE Transactions on Communications*, 23(10): 1142–1147.

Nilles, J.M. 1976. Telecommuting: communications as a substitute for commuting. In: Grunig, J. (ed.), *Decline of the Global Village: How Specialization is Changing the Future of the Mass Media*, New York: General Hall, pp. 137–157.

Nilles, J.M., Carlson, F.G., Gray, P., and Hannemann, G.J. 1976. *The Telecommunications–Transportation Trade-Off: Options for Tomorrow*, New York: Wiley.

Nonaka, I., Toyama, R., and Konno, N. 2000. SECI, Ba and leadership: a unified model of dynamic knowledge creation. *Long Range Planning*, 33(1): 5–34.

OECD. 2021. *The Future of Remote Work: Opportunities and Policy Options for Trentino*, OECD Local Economic and Employment Development (LEED) Papers 2021/07. https://dx.doi.org/10.1787/35f78ced-en.

Offstein, E.H., Morwick, J.M., and Koskinen, L. 2010. Making telework work: leading people and leveraging technology for competitive advantage. *Strategic HR Review*, 9(2): 32–37.

Oldenburg, R. 1989. *The Great Good Place: Cafes, Coffee Shops, Community Centers, Beauty Parlors, General Stores, Bars, Hangouts, and How They Get You Through the Day*, New York: Paragon House.

O'Neill, T.A., Hambley, L.A., and Bercovich, A. 2014. Prediction of cyberslacking when employees are working away from the office. *Computers in Human Behavior*, 34: 291–298.

Overmyer, S.P. 2011. *Implementing Telework: Lessons Learned from Four Federal Agencies*, Arlington, VA: IBM Center for the Business of Government.

Parkinson, J., Schuster, L., and Mulcahy, R. 2022. Online third places: supporting well-being through identifying and managing unintended consequences. *Journal of Service Research*, 25(1): 108–125. https://doi.org/10.1177/10946705211018860.

Parlak, S., Celebi Cakiroglu, O., and Oksuz Gul, F. 2021. Gender roles during COVID-19 pandemic: the experiences of Turkish female academics. *Gender, Work and Organization*, 28(Suppl 2): 461–483.

Pearlson, K.E., and Saunders, C.S. 2001. There's no place like home: managing telecommuting paradoxes. *Academy of Management Executive*, 15(2): 117–128.

Peiró, J.M., and Martínez-Tur, V. 2022. 'Digitalized' competences: a crucial challenge beyond digital competences. *Journal of Work and Organizational Psychology*, 38(3): 189–199. https://doi.org/10.5093/jwop2022a22.

Pérez, M.P., Sánchez, A.M., de Luis Carnicer, P., and Jiménez, M.J.V. 2005. The differences of firm resources and the adoption of teleworking. *Technovation*, 25(12): 1476–1483.

Peters, P., Tijdens, K., and Wetzels, C. 2001. Factors in employees' telecommuting opportunities, preferences and practices. Research Paper No. 008. Paper presented at the 6th International ITF workshop and business conference 'Working in the new economy', Amsterdam, 26–30 August.

Pianese, T., Errichiello, L., and da Cunha, J.V. 2023. Organizational control in the context of remote working: a synthesis of empirical findings and a research agenda. *European Management Review*, 20(2): 326–345. https://doi.org/10.1111/emre.12515.

Pinsonneault, A., and Boisvert, M. 2001. The impacts of telecommuting on organizations and individuals: a review of the literature. In: Johnson, N.J. (ed.), *Telecommuting and Virtual Offices: Issues and Opportunities*, Hershey, PA: Idea Group Publishing, pp. 163–185.

Pyöriä, P. 2011. Managing telework: risks, fears and rules. *Management Research Review*, 34(4): 389–399.

Radoynovska, N., and Ruttan, R. 2021. A matter of transition: authenticity judgments and attracting employees to hybridized organizations. *Organization Science*. https://doi.org/10.1287/orsc.2021.1495.

Raghuram, S., Hill, N.S., Gibbs, J.L., and Maruping, L.M. 2019. Virtual work: bridging research clusters. *Academy of Management Annals*, 13(1): 308–341.

Raghuram, S., Wiesenfeld, B., and Garud, R. 2003. Technology enabled work: the role of self-efficacy in determining telecommuter adjustment and structuring behavior. *Journal of Vocational Behavior*, 63(2): 180–198.

Ravid, D.M., White, J.C., Tomczak, D.L., Miles, A.F., and Behrend, T.S. 2023. A meta-analysis of the effects of electronic performance monitoring on work outcomes. *Personnel Psychology*, 76(1): 5–40. https://doi.org/10.1111/peps.12514.

Reilly, P.A. 1998. Balancing flexibility – meeting the interests of employer and employee. *European Journal of Work and Organizational Psychology*, 7(1): 7–22.

Rhymer, J. 2023. Location-independent organizations: designing collaboration across space and time. *Administrative Science Quarterly*, 68(1): 1–43.

Riedl, R. 2022. On the stress potential of videoconferencing: definition and root causes of Zoom fatigue. *Electronic Markets*, 32(1): 153–177. https://doi.org/10.1007/s12525-021-00501-3.

Risi, E., and Pronzato, R. 2021. Smart working is not so smart: always-on lives and the dark side of platformisation. *Work Organisation, Labour and Globalisation*, 15(1): 107–125. DOI: 10.13169/workorgalaboglob.15.1.0107.

Rousseau, D.M. 1989. Psychological and implied contracts in organizations. *Employee Responsibilities and Rights Journal*, 2: 121–139. https://doi.org/10.1007/BF01384942.

Russell, B. 1945. *A History of Western Philosophy and Its Connections with Political and Social Circumstances from the Earliest Times to the Present Day*, New York: Simon & Schuster.

Salo, M., Pirkkalainen, H., Chua, C.E.H., and Koskelainen, T. 2022. Formation and mitigation of technostress in the personal use of IT. *MIS Quarterly*, 46(2): 1073–1108. https://doi.org/10.25300/MISQ/2022/14950.

Saunders, C., and Ahuja, M. 2006. Are all distributed teams the same? Differentiating between temporary and ongoing distributed teams. *Small Group Research*, 37(6): 662–700.

Schaffers, H., Vartiainen, M., and Bus, J. (eds) 2020. *Digital Innovation and the Future of Work*, Aalborg: River Publishers.

Schaufeli, W.B., and Bakker, A.B. 2004. Job demands, job resources, and their relationship with burnout and engagement: a multi-sample study. *Journal of Organizational Behavior*, 25(3): 293–315. https://doi.org/10.1002/job.248.

Schein, E.H. 1990. Organizational culture. *American Psychologist*, 45(2): 109–119. https://doi.org/10.1037/0003-066X.45.2.109.

Scholz, T. 2013. *Digital Labor: The Internet as Playground and Factory*, New York and London: Routledge.

Schur, L.A., Ameri, M., and Kruse, D. 2020. Telework after COVID: a 'silver lining' for workers with disabilities? *Journal of Occupational Rehabilitation*, 30: 521–536.

Scott, W.R. 1981. *Organizations: Rational, Natural, and Open Systems*, Englewood Cliffs, NJ: Prentice Hall.

Sennett, R. 2006. *The Culture of the New Capitalism*, New Haven, CT and London: Yale University Press.

Shirmohammadi, M., Au, W.C., and Beigi, M. 2022. Remote work and work–life balance: lessons learned from the Covid-19 pandemic and suggestions for HRD practitioners. *Human Resource Development International*, 25(2): 163–181.

Shukla, S.K., Sushil, and Sharma, M.K. 2019. Managerial paradox toward flexibility: emergent views using thematic analysis of literature. *Global Journal of Flexible Systems Management*, 20(4): 349–370.

Smite, D., Christensen, E.L., Tell, P., and Russo, D. 2023. Characterizing the spectrum of hybrid work arrangements for software teams. *IEEE Software*, 40: 34–41. DOI: 10.1109/MS.2022.3230289.

Sostero, M., Milasi, S., Hurley, J., Fernández-Macías, E., and Bisello, M. 2020. *Teleworkability and the COVID-19 crisis: a new digital divide?* European Commission. https://EconPapers.repec.org/RePEc:ipt:laedte:202005.

Stoker, J.I., Garretsen, H., and Lammers, J. 2021. Leading and working from home in times of COVID-19: on the perceived changes in leadership behaviors. *Journal of Leadership and Organizational Studies*, 29(2): 208–218. https://doi.org/10.1177/15480518211007452.

Strack, R., Kovács-Ondrejkovic, O., Baier, J., Antebi, P., Kavanagh, K., and López Gobernado, A. 2021. *Decoding Global Ways of Working*, Boston Consulting Group. https://www.bcg.com/publications/2021/advantages-of-remote-work-flexibility.

Suder, S., and Siibak, A. 2022. Proportionate response to the COVID-19 threat? Use of apps and other technologies for monitoring employees under the European Union's data protection framework. *International Labour Review*, 161(2): 315–335.

Taiwon, Ha 2022. COVID-19 and remote work inequality: evidence from South Korea. *Labor History*, 63(3): 406–420. DOI: 10.1080/0023656X.2022.2111549.

Tannenbaum, S.I., Mathieu, J.E., Salas, E., and Cohen, D. 2012. Teams are changing: are research and practice evolving fast enough? *Industrial and Organizational Psychology*, 5(1): 2–24.

Tarafdar, M., Cooper, C.L., and Stich, F. 2019. The technostress trifecta – techno eustress, techno distress and design: theoretical directions and an agenda for research. *Information Systems* Journal, 29(1): 6–42. https://doi.org/10.1111/isj.12169.

Taylor, S.E. 2011. Social support: a review. In: Friedman, M.S. (ed.), *The Handbook of Health Psychology*, Oxford: Oxford University Press, pp. 189–214.

Teevan, J., Baym, N., Butler, J., Hecht, B., Jaffe, S., Nowak, K., Sellen, A., and Yang, L. (eds). 2022. *Microsoft New Future of Work Report 2022*, Microsoft Research Tech Report MSR-TR-2022-3. https://aka.ms/nfw2022.

Tessarini, G., Saltorato, P., and Da Silva Rosa, K.L. 2023. Flexible work as a rule in capitalism: conceptualization and theoretical-analytical propositions, *Cad. EBAPE. BR*, 21(1): 1–13. https://doi.org/10.1590/1679-395120220049x.

Thielsch, M., Röseler, S., Kirsch, J., Lamers, C., and Hertel, G. 2020. Managing pandemics – demands, resources, and effective behaviors within crisis management teams. *Applied Psychology: An International Review*, 70(1): 150–187.

Tims, M., Bakker, A.B., and Derks, D. 2012. Development and validation of the job crafting scale. *Journal of Vocational Behavior*, 80(1): 173–186. doi:10.1016/j.jvb.2011.05.009.

Toffler, A. 1980. *The Third Wave*, London: William Collins & Sons.

Tredinnick, L., and Laybats, C. 2021. Blended workplaces. *Business Information Review*, 38(3): 108–110.

Tregaskis, O., Brewster, C., Mayne, L., and Hegewisch, A. 1998. Flexible working in Europe: the evidence and the implications. *European Journal of Work and Organizational Psychology*, 7(1): 61–78.

Tremblay, D.G., and Thomsin, L. 2012. Telework and mobile working: analysis of its benefits and drawbacks. *International Journal of Work Innovation*, 1(1): 100–113.

Van den Broeck, A., De Cuyper, N., De Witte, H., and Vansteenkiste, M. 2010. Not all job demands are equal: differentiating job hindrances and job challenges in the Job Demands–Resources model. *European Journal of Work and Organizational Psychology*, 19(6): 735–759.

Van Eyck, K. 2003. *Flexibilizing Employment: An Overview*, Geneva: International Labour Office.

Van Yperen, N.W., Rietzschel, E.F., and De Jonge, K.M.M. 2014. Blended working: for whom it may (not) work. *PLoS ONE*, 9(7): e102921. doi:10.1371/journal.ponc.0102921.

van Zoonen, W., Sivunen, A., Blomqvist, K., Olsson, T., Ropponen, A., Henttonen, K., and Vartiainen, M. 2021. Factors influencing adjustment to remote work: employees' initial responses to the COVID-19 pandemic. *International Journal of Environmental Research and Public Health*, 18(13): 6966.

Vartiainen, M. 2007. Distributed and mobile workplaces. In: Vartiainen, M., Hakonen, M., Koivisto, S., Mannonen, P., Nieminen, M.P., Ruohomäki, V., and Vartola, A. (eds), *Distributed and Mobile Work – Places, People and Technology*, Helsinki: Otatieto, pp. 13–85.

Vartiainen, M. 2020. Competencies in digital work. In: Schaffers, H., Vartiainen, M., and Bus, J. (eds), *Digital Innovation and the Future of Work*, Aalborg: River Publishers, pp. 225–257.

Vartiainen, M.A. 2021. Telework and remote work. In: Peiró, J.M. (ed.), *Oxford Research Encyclopedia of Psychology*, Oxford: Oxford University Press. https://doi.org/10.1093/acrefore/9780190236557.013.850.
Vartiainen, M. 2023. Dual role of leadership in 'Janus-faced' telework from home. In: Bergum, S., Peters, P., and Vold, T. (eds), *Virtual Management and the New Normal: New Perspectives on HRM and Leadership since the COVID-19*, Basingstoke: Palgrave Macmillan, pp. 269–289. https://doi.org/10.1007/978-3-031-06813-3_14.
Vartiainen, M., and Hyrkkänen, U. 2010. Changing requirements and mental workload factors in mobile multi-locational work. *New Technology, Work and Employment*, 25(2): 117–135.
Vartiainen, M., and Vanharanta, O. 2023. *Hybrid Work: Definition, Origins, Debates and Outlook*, Working paper, No. WPEF23002, European Foundation for the Improvement of Living and Working Conditions. https://www.eurofound.europa.eu/sites/default/files/wpef23002.pdf.
Vartiainen, M., Hakonen, M., Koivisto, S., Mannonen, P., Nieminen, M., Ruohomäki, V., and Vartola, A. 2007. *Distributed and Mobile Work: Places, People and Technology*, Helsinki: Otatieto.
Venkatesh, V., and Johnson, P. 2002. Social richness, telepresence, and user acceptance: a longitudinal field study of telecommuting technology implementations. *Personnel Psychology*, 55(3): 661–688.
Venz, L., and Boettcher, K. 2021. Leading in times of crisis: how perceived COVID-19-related work intensification links to daily e-mail demands and leader outcomes. *Applied Psychology*, 1–23. https://doi.org/10.1111/apps.12357.
Verelst, L., De Cooman, R., and Verbruggen, M. 2023. Crafting when teleworking: a daily diary study on the combinations of job and home crafting and their relationship with energy depletion. *Journal of Vocational Behavior*, 143: 103880. https://doi.org/10.1016/j.jvb.2023.103880.
Wageman, R., Gardner, H., and Mortensen, M. 2012. The changing ecology of teams: new directions for teams research. *Journal of Organizational Behavior*, 33(3): 301–315.
Wang, B., Liu, Y., Qian, J., and Parker, S. 2020. Achieving effective remote working during the COVID-19 pandemic: a work design perspective. *Applied Psychology: An International Review*, 70(1): 16–59.
Wessels, C., Schippers, M.C., Stegmann, S., Bakker, A.B., van Baalen, P.J., and Proper, K.I. 2019. Fostering flexibility in the new world of work: a model of time-spatial job crafting. *Frontiers in Psychology*, 10: 505. doi: 10.3389/fpsyg.2019.00505.
West, B.J., Patera, J.L., and Carsten, M.K. 2009. Team level positivity: investigating positive psychological capacities and team level outcomes. *Journal of Organizational Behavior*, 30(2): 249–267.
Wheatley, D., Broome, M.R., Dobbins, T., Hopkins, B., and Powell, O. 2023. Navigating choppy water: flexibility ripple effects in the COVID-19 pandemic and the future of remote and hybrid working. *Work, Employment and Society*. https://doi.org/10.1177/09500170231195230.
White, M., Hill, S., McGovern, P., Mills, C., and Smeaton, D. 2003. 'High-performance' management practices, working hours and work–life balance. *British Journal of Industrial Relations*, 41(2): 175–195.
Wigert, B. 2022. *The Future of Hybrid Work: 5 Key Questions Answered with Data*, Gallup. https://www.gallup.com/workplace/390632/future-hybrid-work-key-questions-answered-data.aspx.

Yang, L., Holtz, D., Jaffe, S., Suri, S., Sinha, S., Weston, J., et al. 2022. The effects of remote work on collaboration among information workers. *Nature Human Behaviour*, 6(January): 43–54. www.nature.com/nathumbehav.

Yee, N., and Bailenson, J. 2007. The Proteus effect: the effect of transformed self-representation on behavior. *Human Communication Research*, 33(3): 271–290. https://doi.org/10.1111/j.1468-2958.2007.00299.x.

Index